SEC

# TOUCHSTONE

## WORKBOOK 2

MICHAEL MCCARTHY
JEANNE MCCARTEN
HELEN SANDIFORD

CAMBRIDGE
UNIVERSITY PRESS

University Printing House, Cambridge CB2 8BS, United Kingdom

One Liberty Plaza, 20th Floor, New York, NY 10006, USA

477 Williamstown Road, Port Melbourne, VIC 3207, Australia

4843/24, 2nd Floor, Ansari Road, Daryaganj, Delhi – 110002, India

79 Anson Road, #06–04/06, Singapore 079906

Cambridge University Press is part of the University of Cambridge.

It furthers the University's mission by disseminating knowledge in the pursuit of education, learning, and research at the highest international levels of excellence.

www.cambridge.org
Information on this title: www.cambridge.org/9781107690370



First published 2005
Second Edition 2014
20 19 18 17 16 15 14 13 12

Printed in Malaysia by Vivar Printing

*A catalog record for this publication is available from the British Library.*

ISBN 978-1-107-68173-6 Student's Book
ISBN 978-1-107-68175-0 Student's Book A
ISBN 978-1-107-62704-8 Student's Book B
ISBN 978-1-107-69037-0 Workbook
ISBN 978-1-107-64988-0 Workbook A
ISBN 978-1-107-61861-9 Workbook B
ISBN 978-1-107-65940-7 Full Contact
ISBN 978-1-107-61439-0 Full Contact A
ISBN 978-1-107-66547-7 Full Contact B
ISBN 978-1-107-62402-3 Teacher's Edition with Assessment Audio CD/CD-ROM
ISBN 978-1-107-67757-9 Class Audio CDs (4)

Additional resources for this publication at www.cambridge.org/touchstone2

# Contents

# Making friends

UNIT 1

## Lesson A Getting to know you

### 1 About you 1

Grammar and vocabulary

**A Complete the chart with the words in the box.**

| | | | |
|---|---|---|---|
| college | major | ✓neighborhood | parents |
| job | movies | only child | TV |

| Home and family | School and work | Free time and friends |
|---|---|---|
| *neighborhood* | | |
| | | |
| | | |

**B Answer the questions with your own information. Use short answers.**

1. Are you an only child? *Yes, I am.* **or** *No, I'm not.*
2. Is your neighborhood quiet? ____________
3. Do you live with your parents? ____________
4. Do you have a big TV? ____________
5. Do you and your friends go to college? ____________
6. Are you a French major? ____________
7. Does your best friend like action movies? ____________
8. Is homework fun? ____________

### 2 You and me

Grammar **Complete the conversation with the verb *be*. Use contractions where possible.**

**Koji** Hi. *I'm* Koji.
**Isabel** Hi. I ________ Isabel. Where ________ you from, Koji?
**Koji** I ________ from Japan. How about you?
**Isabel** Monterrey – in Mexico.
**Koji** Oh, my friends Manuel and Rosa ________ from Mexico, too.
**Isabel** Really? ________ they here now?
**Koji** No, they ________ not. Uh, I guess they ________ late.
**Isabel** ________ the teacher here?
**Koji** Yes, she ________ . She ________ over there.
**Isabel** She looks nice. What ________ her name?
**Koji** I think it ________ Ms. Barnes.

## 3 I'm Rudy.

Grammar | **Answer the questions. Write another piece of information.**

1. Is Rudy from San Francisco?
   *No, he's not. He's from Los Angeles.*
2. Are his friends English majors?
   ______________________

3. Do his friends study in the evening?
   ______________________
4. Does Rudy live alone?
   ______________________

## About you 2

Grammar and vocabulary | **Unscramble the questions. Then answer the questions with your own information.**

1. name / What's / first / your ? *What's your first name?*
   ______________________
2. full-time / a / Do / have / you / job ? ______________________
   ______________________
3. live / best friend / Does / your / nearby ? ______________________
   ______________________
4. weekends / What / do / on / you / do ? ______________________
   ______________________
5. does / your neighbor / What / for a living / do ? ______________________
   ______________________
6. live / Do / alone / you ? ______________________
   ______________________

## 1 What doesn't belong?

Vocabulary | **Circle the word that doesn't belong in each group.**

1. apples (butter) mangoes strawberries
2. TV jacket jeans sweater
3. black color green red
4. baseball basketball singing volleyball
5. cat dog fish pet
6. dessert juice milk water

## 2 We're the same.

Grammar | **Respond to the statements with *too* or *either*.**

1. I'm a soccer fan.
*I am too.*

2. I can't stand doing the laundry.
_______________

3. I can sing karaoke all night.
_______________

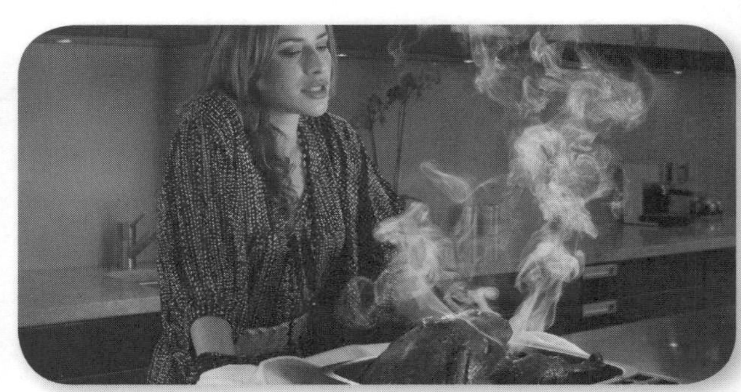

4. I'm not a good cook.
_______________

5. I don't like shopping.
_______________

6. I love to swim in cold water.
_______________

## 3 First date

Grammar and vocabulary

**Complete the conversations with the expressions in the box. You can use some expressions more than once.**

| ✓I am too. | I do too. | I can too. |
|---|---|---|
| I'm not either. | I don't either. | I can't either. |

David You know, I'm always nervous on first dates.

Lesley *I am too.* I guess I'm not very outgoing.

David I guess ___ So, what do you like to do in your free time?

Lesley Well, I go to rock concerts.

David ___ I'm a big fan of Kings of Leon.

Lesley ___ They're my favorite group. I mean, I can listen to their music for hours.

David ___ Do you have all their songs?

Lesley No, I don't. I don't have *The End*.

David ___ But I want to buy it.

Lesley What do you do on the weekends? I mean, do you eat out a lot?

David No. I don't usually go to restaurants.

Lesley ___ I like to eat at home.

David Oh, are you a good cook?

Lesley Um, no. I can't say I'm a good cook.

David ___ But I like to cook.

Lesley Do you ever cook Italian food?

David Sure. I love pasta and pizza.

Lesley ___

David That's amazing! We have a lot in common. Do you like sports? I'm a big sports fan. I watch sports all weekend.

Lesley Oh . . .

## 4 About you

Grammar and vocabulary

**Respond to these statements so they are true for you.**

1. A I always eat chocolate after dinner.
   B *I do too.* **or** *Me too.* **or** *Really? I don't.*
2. A I'm not a baseball fan.
   B ___
3. A I can't drive.
   B ___
4. A I don't have a pet.
   B ___
5. A I'm allergic to bananas.
   B ___
6. A I can cook Italian food.
   B ___

# Lesson C It's cold tonight.

## 1 Starting a conversation

Conversation strategies **Complete the conversations with the conversation starters in the box.**

| | |
|---|---|
| Is this your first English class here? | You look really nice today. That's a beautiful jacket. |
| Hi. Are you new here? Do you live around here? | Boy, the food is great. And this cake is really wonderful. |
| Is it me, or is it kind of noisy in here? | ✓ Oh, it's cold. Can I close the window? |

1. A *Oh, it's cold. Can I close the window?*
   B Sorry, I just opened it. I'm a little warm, actually.

2. A ______________________
   B Thanks. Actually, it's from China.

3. A ______________________
   B Thank you. It's my grandmother's recipe.

4. A ______________________
   B Yes, it is. Are you in this class, too?

5. A ______________________
   B Yeah, it's pretty loud! Is this your first time here?

6. A ______________________
   B Uh, no, I don't. I'm actually visiting from Guadalajara.

## 2 Um, actually, . . .

Conversation strategies

**Match each conversation starter with a response.**

1. It's really hot in here. _b_
2. Do you know anyone in this class? ____
3. Do you live in this neighborhood? ____
4. Do you walk to class? ____
5. I like your necklace. ____
6. Do you like coffee? ____

a. Yes, most days. It's actually only five minutes from work.
✓b. It often gets hot in here. But I feel OK today, actually.
c. No, um actually, . . . I'm a little shy.
d. Thanks. It's actually from Colombia.
e. Actually, no, but I work near here.
f. Yeah, I do. Actually, there's a great coffee shop across the street.

## 3 First day of class

Conversation strategies

**Imagine it's the first day of English class. Respond to each conversation starter.**

1. I don't know anyone here. — _I don't either, actually. By the way, I'm James._
2. I feel a little nervous. — ____
3. Is it warm in here, or is it me? — ____
4. I don't know the teacher's name. — ____
5. Are you a friend of Sara's? — ____
6. I really like your bag. — ____
7. What time does the class finish? — ____
8. Do we get a break? — ____
9. This is a nice classroom. — ____
10. Can we use dictionaries, do you think? — ____

# Lesson D Making small talk

## 1 Getting together

Reading **A Read the article. Which of these are good suggestions for making small talk? Check (✓) the boxes.**

- ☐ Don't look at the other person.
- ☐ Keep quiet when the other person is talking.
- ☐ Ask questions that start with *what*, *where*, *how*, or *when*.
- ☐ Have some good topics to discuss.
- ☐ Talk about yourself a lot.

Social Conversations

### Eight Tips for Great Social Conversations

Are you shy? Do you find conversations with new people difficult? If you do, then these eight tips can help you connect. If you're outgoing and love to talk, they can help you improve your conversation skills.

1 **Have some topics ready to start a conversation.** Say something about the weather or the place you're in. Talk about the weekend – we all have something to say about weekends!

2 **Make the conversation interesting.** Know about events in the news. Read restaurant and movie reviews. Find out about the current music scene or what's new in fashion or sports.

3 **Be a good listener.** Make eye contact and say, "Yes," "Hmm," "Uh-huh," "Right," and "I know." And say, "Really? That's interesting." It encourages people to talk.

4 **Don't be boring.** Don't just say, "Yes" or "No" when you answer a question. Give some interesting details, too.

5 **Don't talk all the time.** Ask, "How about you?" and show you are interested in the other person, too. People love to talk about themselves!

6 **Ask information questions.** Ask questions like, "What do you do in your free time?" or "What kind of food do you like?" Use follow-up questions to keep the conversation going. But don't ask too many questions – it's not an interview!

7 **Be positive.** Negative comments can sound rude. And if you don't want to answer a personal question, simply say, "Oh, I'm not sure I can answer that," or "I'd rather not say."

8 **Smile!** Everyone loves a smile. Just be relaxed, smile, and be yourself.

**B Read the article again and circle the correct words.**

1. It's **good** / **not good** to make short responses when you listen.
2. When you answer questions, **you can say** / **don't just reply** "Yes" or "No."
3. Ask **a couple of** / **a lot of** follow-up questions.
4. **Think** / **Don't think** of a conversation like an interview.
5. You **have to** / **don't have to** answer personal questions.

# 2 Suggestions, please!

Writing **A Rewrite Ben's email to a magazine and the problem page editor's reply. Use correct punctuation.**

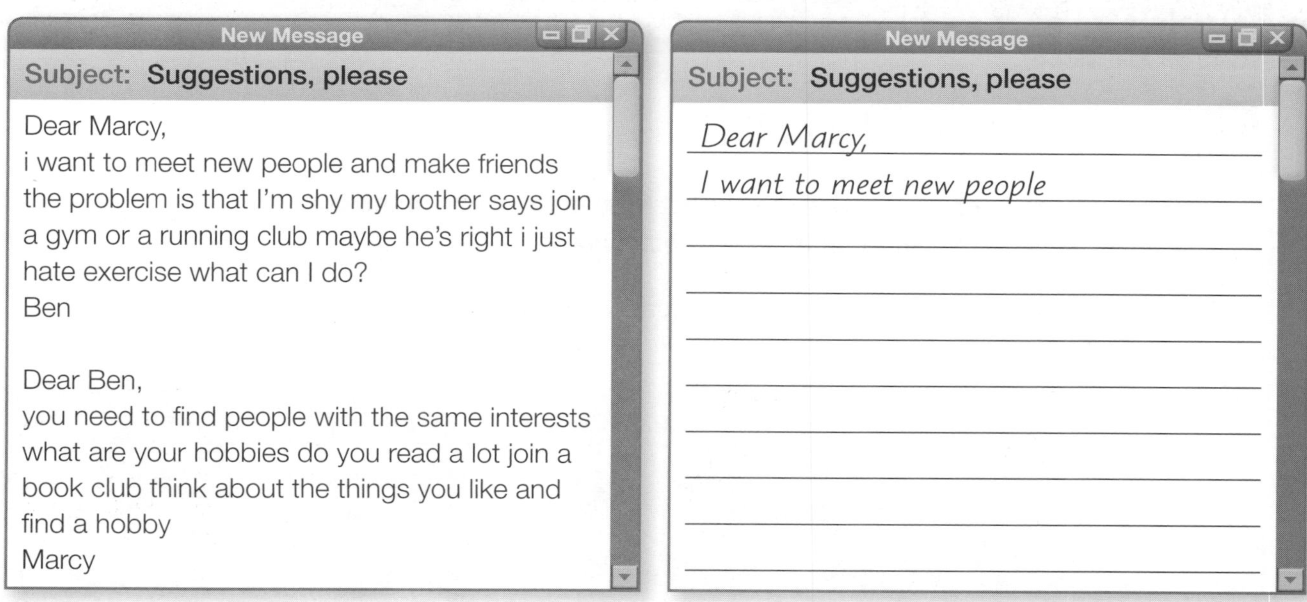
New Message

Subject: Suggestions, please

Dear Marcy,
i want to meet new people and make friends the problem is that I'm shy my brother says join a gym or a running club maybe he's right i just hate exercise what can I do?
Ben

Dear Ben,
you need to find people with the same interests what are your hobbies do you read a lot join a book club think about the things you like and find a hobby
Marcy

New Message

Subject: Suggestions, please

*Dear Marcy,*
*I want to meet new people* ____________

______________________________

______________________________

______________________________

______________________________

______________________________

______________________________

______________________________

______________________________

**B Read these questions. Write three suggestions for each question.**

1. ***Dave*** I'd like to make friends, but I don't know how. Do you have any suggestions?

______________________________

______________________________

2. ***Niki*** I feel shy around new people. How can I improve my conversation skills?

______________________________

______________________________

## Unit 1 Progress chart

| | **What can you do? Mark the boxes.** ✓ = I can . . . ? = I need to review how to . . . | To review, go back to these pages in the Student's Book. |
|---|---|---|
| Grammar | ☐ make statements with the simple present and present of *be*.<br>☐ ask questions with the simple present and present of *be*.<br>☐ use *too* and *either* to agree. | 2, 3, 4, and 5<br>2 and 3<br>4 and 5 |
| Vocabulary | ☐ use at least 20 words to describe home and family, school and work, and free time and friends. | 2 and 3 |
| Conversation strategies | ☐ start conversations with people I don't know.<br>☐ use *actually* to give and "correct" information. | 6 and 7<br>7 |
| Writing | ☐ use capital letters, commas, quotation marks, question marks, and periods. | 9 |

# Interests

UNIT 2

## Lesson A Leisure time

### 1 What do they like to do?

Grammar **Complete the sentences. Use the correct form of the verbs in the box. Sometimes there is more than one correct answer.**

| cook | dance | draw | play | ✓read | work out |
|---|---|---|---|---|---|

1. Pam and Victor aren't interested in _reading_ books. They both prefer _to read_ magazines. They really enjoy _reading_ fashion magazines.

2. Ian would like ________ every day. He doesn't like ________ in the gym. He enjoys ________ at home.

3. Sun Hee can't ________ . She's interested in ________ and would like ________ the tango.

4. Tom isn't good at ________ people. He hates ________ people, but he can ________ animals very well.

5. Amy and Dave usually like ________ , but they can't ________ Italian food. They prefer ________ Chinese food.

6. Erica can't ________ the guitar very well. She enjoys ________ music, but she's not very good at ________ it.

## 2 At home

Grammar **Complete the sentences. Use the correct form of the verbs in the box. Sometimes there is more than one correct answer.**

| bowl | go | ski | try |
|---|---|---|---|
| ✓exercise | play | swim | watch |

**Linda** You and I watch too much TV. We need some exercise.
**James** I know, but I don't really enjoy *exercising* .
**Linda** But you like ________ tennis, right?
**James** Yeah, but these days I prefer ________ tennis on TV.
**Linda** How about bowling? You're good at ________ .
**James** Yeah, but it's always noisy at the bowling alley.
**Linda** I guess you're right.
**James** Well, we can both ________ . And the pool's nearby.
**Linda** But it's always crowded.
**James** Oh, I know! We both like ________ .
**Linda** Actually, I can't stand the cold and snow.
**James** Really? Well, are you interested in ________ something new?
**Linda** Sure. I'd like ________ to the new Thai restaurant in our neighborhood.
**James** Great idea, Linda. Let's think about exercising tomorrow.

## 3 About you

Grammar and vocabulary **Answer the questions with true information. Add more information.**

1. A What are you good at?
   B *Well, I'm pretty good at learning languages. I can speak Portuguese and French.*
2. A What are you bad at?
   B ________________________________
3. A Would you like to play a musical instrument?
   B ________________________________
4. A What movie do you want to see?
   B ________________________________
5. A What do you really hate doing?
   B ________________________________
6. A What do you enjoy doing on the weekends?
   B ________________________________

## 1 All kinds of music

Vocabulary | **Look at the pictures. Write the type of music.**

1. *folk music*
2. j ____________
3. r ____________
4. l ____________
5. c ____________
6. c ____________
7. p ____________
8. r ____________

## 2 What's new?

Grammar | **Complete Kevin's email with the correct words.**

New Message

To: Sam_P@cup.com
From: KevinJ@cup.com
Subject: My new job

Hi Sam,

Guess what! I have a new job at a café. They play some great music here so it's a great job for ___*me*___ (me / it). I really like __________ (him / it).

They play music by some great bands, like Maroon 5. Do you know __________ (her / them)? Then there's Bruno Mars. He's cool. I really like __________ (him / it), too. Actually, I think almost everybody in the café __________ (is / are) a Bruno Mars fan. Do you like country music? I don't really care for __________ (it / him). No one I know really __________ (like / likes) country. But I think Taylor Swift is cool, and she has a great new album. Do you know __________ (us / her)?

Oh, did I tell you? I'm in a band with some friends at the café. They're really great. I want you to meet __________ (him / them). We play hip-hop. But no one in my family __________ (come / comes) to listen to __________ (him / us). They don't like hip-hop! But that's OK.

What's new with you? Write soon.

Kevin

## 3 Talking about music

Grammar **Complete the questions with object pronouns. Then answer the questions.**

1. A Beyoncé's a great singer. She's pretty, too.
   Do you like *her* ?
   B *Yes, I do. She's amazing.*
2. A You know Justin Timberlake, right? I think he's great.
   What do you think of ________ ?
   B ________________________
3. A You know, I'm not a fan of jazz. How about you?
   Do you ever listen to ________ ?
   B ________________________
4. A Hey, the Black Keys were on TV last night. They're a really cool band. Do you know ________ ?
   B ________________________
5. A My mom and dad love Sarah Chang. She's their favorite violinist. Do your parents like ________ ?
   B ________________________
6. A Do you like Latin music? Jeff and I have tickets for the Shakira concert. Do you want to go with ________ ?
   B ________________________
7. A I don't usually like country bands, but I love Lady Antebellum.
   Do you know ________ ?
   B ________________________

## 4 About you

Grammar and vocabulary **Answer the questions using object pronouns. Then give more information.**

1. Do you like Alicia Keys? *Yes, I like her a lot. She has some great songs.* **or**
   *Actually, I don't know her.*
2. What do you think of the Rolling Stones? ________________________
3. Do you like Mariah Carey? ________________________
4. Do you listen to pop music very often? ________________________
5. What do you think of folk music? ________________________
6. Do you and your friends ever go to concerts? ________________________
7. What do you think of Bruno Mars? ________________________
8. Do you know the band The Lumineers? ________________________

# Lesson C / I'm not really into it.

## 1 Saying *no*

Conversation strategies | **Complete the conversations with the sentences in the box.**

| | |
|---|---|
| Not really. He just watches TV a lot. | ✓ Not really. My mom knitted it for me last year. |
| Actually, no. My sister got it at the bakery. | No, but he collects caps. |
| Well, no. I like to make peanut butter cookies. | No. I'm not really good with my hands. |
| Um, no. He just uses it for computer games. | Not really. Well, I guess his computer is a hobby. |

1. Jenny I really like your sweater. Is it new?
   Keiko *Not really. My mom knitted it for me last year.*
   Jenny It's really nice. So, can you knit, too?
   Keiko ______________________ But I bake a little.
   Jenny Oh, did you make this cake?
   Keiko ______________________
   But I like to make cookies sometimes.
   Jenny Me too. Do you ever make chocolate chip cookies?
   Keiko ______________________
   My new boyfriend loves them!

2. Mike I want to buy a Yankees baseball cap for my brother.
   Greg Why? Is it his birthday?
   Mike ______________________
   Does your brother collect anything?
   Greg My brother? ______________________
   Mike But he can't watch it all the time. Does he have any hobbies?
   Greg ______________________
   Mike Oh, yeah? My brother is on the computer all the time.
   Greg Oh, does he use it for homework?
   Mike ______________________

## 2 No, not really.

Conversation strategies | **Complete the responses to make them more friendly.**

1. A Do you go online a lot?
   B Not really. *I don't have a computer.*
2. A What a great photo! Are you interested in photography?
   B No. ______________________
3. A I really enjoy my piano lessons. Would you like to learn to play the piano?
   B Um, no. ______________________
4. A I love growing flowers and vegetables. Do you enjoy gardening?
   B Well, not really. ______________________

## 3 Yes and no

Conversation strategies | **Answer the questions in a friendly way. Use *really* in each answer.**

1. A Are you good at fixing things?
   B No, *not really. I'm not good with my hands* .
   C Yes, *I'm really good at fixing cars* .

2. A Do you make your own clothes?
   B No, ________________ .
   C Yes, ________________ .

3. A Does your best friend collect anything?
   B No, ________________ .
   C Yes, ________________ .

4. A Does your teacher speak Russian?
   B No, ________________ .
   C Yes, ________________ .

5. A Are you into winter sports, like skiing?
   B No, ________________ .
   C Yes, ________________ .

6. A Do you and your friends enjoy cooking?
   B Um, no, ________________ .
   C Yes, ________________ .

7. A Are your classmates into computer games?
   B No, ________________ .
   C Yes, ________________ .

8. A Are you interested in photography?
   B No, ________________ .
   C Yes, ________________ .

## 4 About you

Conversation strategies | **Answer the questions with your own information. Use *really* in your answers.**

1. Are you into sports?
   *Yes, I really like soccer and volleyball.* **or** *No, not really. I prefer doing artistic things.*

2. Would you like to learn a new language?
   ________________

3. Do you have a lot of hobbies?
   ________________

4. Can you knit or sew?
   ________________

5. Are you artistic?
   ________________

# Lesson D Online forums

## 1 Popular interests

Reading **A Read the online forum posts. Write the correct topic for each post.**

| ✓Cooking | Music | Photography | Running | Water sports |
|---|---|---|---|---|
| Fashion | Pets | Reading | Technology | Winter sports |

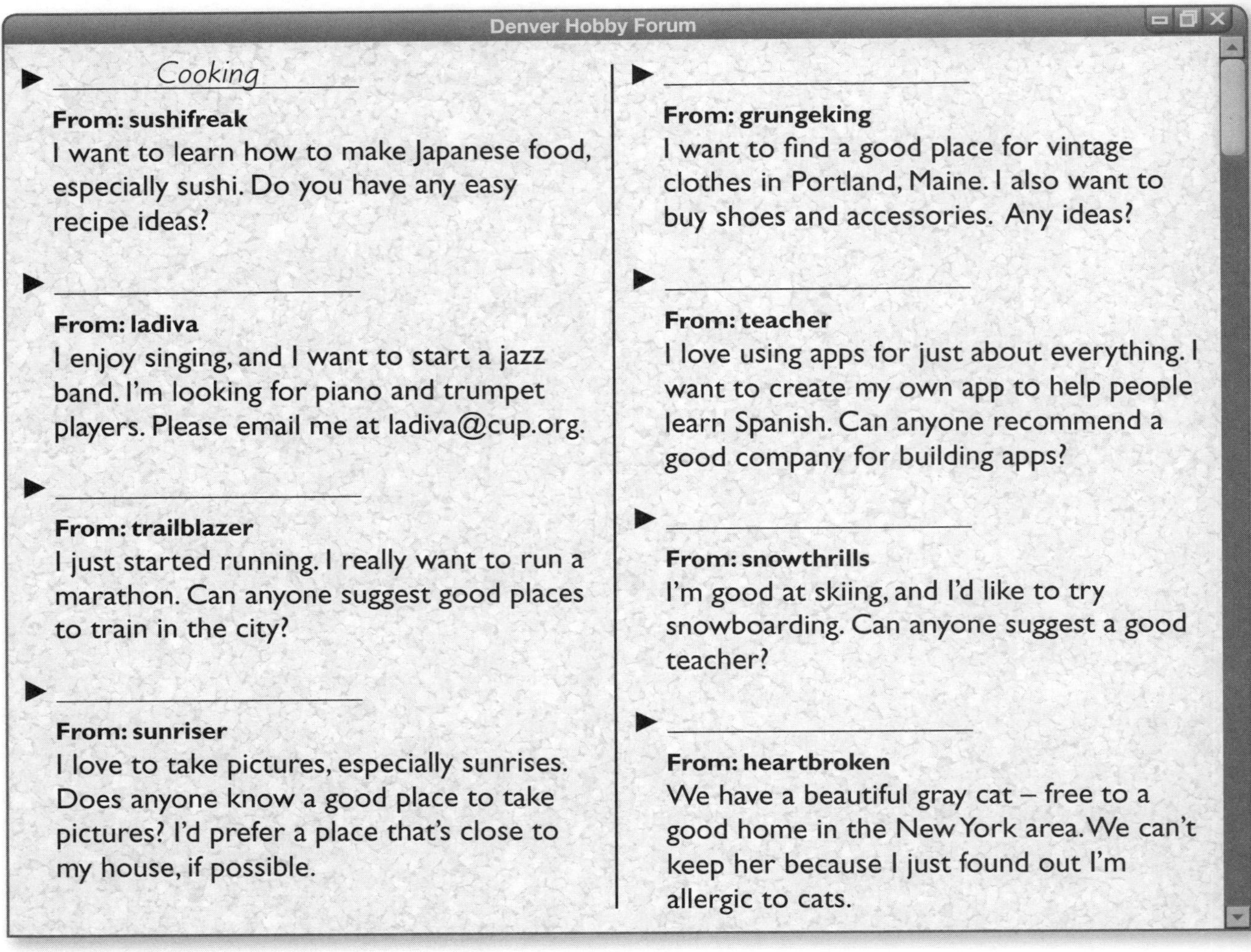

Denver Hobby Forum

▶ Cooking

**From: sushifreak**
I want to learn how to make Japanese food, especially sushi. Do you have any easy recipe ideas?

▶ ______

**From: ladiva**
I enjoy singing, and I want to start a jazz band. I'm looking for piano and trumpet players. Please email me at ladiva@cup.org.

▶ ______

**From: trailblazer**
I just started running. I really want to run a marathon. Can anyone suggest good places to train in the city?

▶ ______

**From: sunriser**
I love to take pictures, especially sunrises. Does anyone know a good place to take pictures? I'd prefer a place that's close to my house, if possible.

▶ ______

**From: grungeking**
I want to find a good place for vintage clothes in Portland, Maine. I also want to buy shoes and accessories. Any ideas?

▶ ______

**From: teacher**
I love using apps for just about everything. I want to create my own app to help people learn Spanish. Can anyone recommend a good company for building apps?

▶ ______

**From: snowthrills**
I'm good at skiing, and I'd like to try snowboarding. Can anyone suggest a good teacher?

▶ ______

**From: heartbroken**
We have a beautiful gray cat – free to a good home in the New York area. We can't keep her because I just found out I'm allergic to cats.

**B Read the responses to the posts below. Who are they for? Match the responses with the writers of the posts. Write *a* to *h*.**

1. I like to run the track at Livingston Park. c
2. IceCat Technology makes good software. ____
3. I'm pretty good at playing the piano. Let's jam! ____
4. We'd love to have her! We live in Bergen County. ____
5. I take pictures at Keystone Park. It has great views. ____
6. Try www.50s.cup.com. They have great 1950s dresses and stuff. ____
7. I can send you my recipe for *kayu*. It's delicious! ____
8. Call the ski resort and ask for an experienced instructor. ____

a. teacher
b. heartbroken
✓c. trailblazer
d. snowthrills
e. sushifreak
f. ladiva
g. sunriser
h. grungeking

# 2 My favorite hobby

Writing

**A Complete the post with *and*, *but*, *or*, *also*, *because*, or *especially*. Sometimes there is more than one correct answer.**

Message Board

### Rock climbing

One of my hobbies is rock climbing. I go once or twice a month with my family ___or___ friends. We like to climb the mountains near my house _________ they're really beautiful _________ the views are wonderful. We often go to Bear Mountain _________ Kennedy Park. I prefer Kennedy Park _________ it's closer. Kennedy Park _________ has a great campground.

It's great to be outdoors, _________ the weather isn't always very good. When it's raining _________ snowing, climbing can be very dangerous _________ the rocks get wet and slippery.

In the winter, my friends _________ I sometimes go rock climbing indoors, usually on a Saturday _________ Sunday. There's a climbing wall at the mall, _________ it's not the same. We prefer to be outdoors, _________ in the summer.

**B Write about one of your hobbies.**

*One of my hobbies is*

## Unit 2 Progress chart

| What can you do? Mark the boxes.<br>✓ = I can . . . ? = I need to review how to . . . | To review, go back to these pages in the Student's Book. |
|---|---|
| **Grammar** | |
| ☐ make statements with different verb forms. | 12 and 13 |
| ☐ ask questions with different verb forms. | 12 and 13 |
| ☐ use the correct verb forms after other verbs, modal verbs, and prepositions. | 12 and 13 |
| ☐ use object pronouns, and the pronouns *everybody* and *nobody*. | 15 |
| **Vocabulary** | |
| ☐ name at least 8 common interests. | 12 and 13 |
| ☐ name at least 8 hobbies. | 12, 13, 16, and 17 |
| ☐ name at least 8 kinds of music. | 14 and 15 |
| **Conversation strategies** | |
| ☐ say *no* in a polite and friendly way. | 16 and 17 |
| ☐ use *really* and *not really* to make statements stronger or softer. | 17 |
| **Writing** | |
| ☐ use *and*, *but*, *or*, *also*, *especially*, or *because* to link ideas. | 19 |

# Health

UNIT 3

## Lesson A Healthy living

### 1 Staying in shape

Grammar | **Complete the conversations with the correct form of the verbs.**

1. Max Hi, Carl. How ___is___ it ___going___ (go)?
   Carl Great. What ________ you ________ (do)?
   Max Oh. I ________ (try) to get in shape before graduation.
   Carl So ________ you ________ (try) to lose weight?
   Max Yeah, a little. I ________ (want) to look good in the photo. So this month I ________ (exercise) and ________ (eat) salads. And I ________ (cut) down on fried food and things like that.
   Carl Good for you. You know, I ________ (read) an interesting book about healthy eating right now. ________ you ________ (want) to borrow it?
   Max Sure. Thanks. But you always ________ (look) so good. You ________ (not need) to lose weight.
   Carl Well, it's probably because I usually ________ (eat) healthy foods and I ________ (exercise) most days.

2. Doctor So, Paul, you ________ (want) to improve your lifestyle.
   Paul Yes, I ________ (need) to get into shape. I know I ________ (not get) enough exercise right now, but I ________ (not have) the energy.
   Doctor So, what exercise ________ you ________ (do) these days?
   Paul Actually, I ________ (not get) any exercise at all. I ________ (work) on a big project for my job, and I ________ (not have) a lot of time. Life's kind of stressful right now.
   Doctor So how ________ you usually ________ (cope) with stress?
   Paul Well, right now, I ________ (not cope) really. Usually I ________ (not eat) a lot of snacks and chocolate, but I ________ (eat) a lot of them now.
   Doctor So ________ you usually ________ (have) a healthy diet?
   Paul Well, it's not bad, I guess. I ________ (love) red meat, and I ________ (eat) that every day. I ________ really ________ (not like) vegetables, so I ________ often ________ (not eat) them.
   Doctor Well, I think you ________ (need) to eat a balanced diet and to get more exercise. Try this plan for four weeks. Then come back in two weeks so we can review it.
   Paul OK. Thanks.

## 2 Susan's lifestyle

Grammar | **Look at the picture and complete the email with the correct form of the verbs in the box.**

| do | drink | drink | eat | have | not buy | not do | not try | play | want | ✓work out |
|---|---|---|---|---|---|---|---|---|---|---|

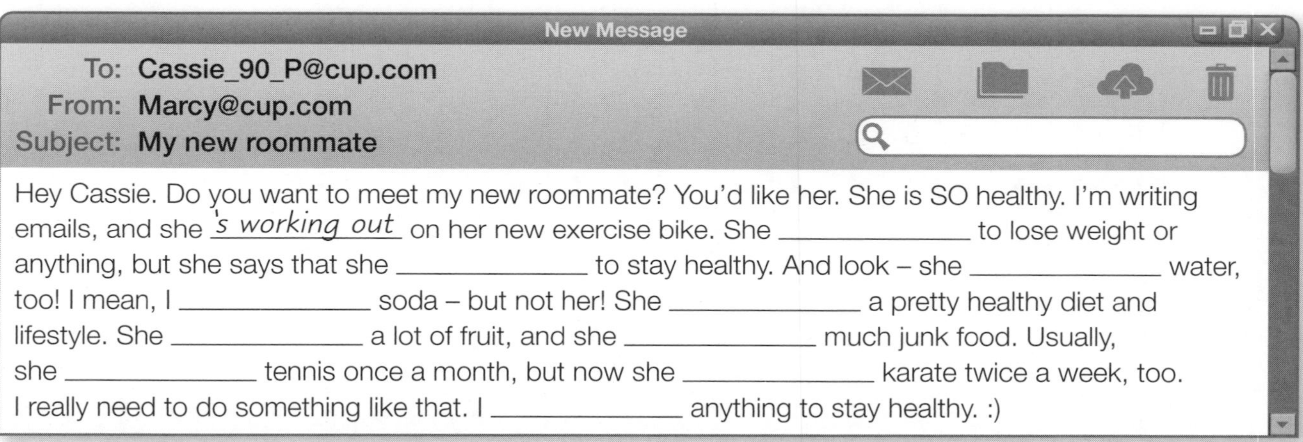

New Message

To: Cassie_90_P@cup.com
From: Marcy@cup.com
Subject: My new roommate

Hey Cassie. Do you want to meet my new roommate? You'd like her. She is SO healthy. I'm writing emails, and she *'s working out* on her new exercise bike. She ______ to lose weight or anything, but she says that she ______ to stay healthy. And look – she ______ water, too! I mean, I ______ soda – but not her! She ______ a pretty healthy diet and lifestyle. She ______ a lot of fruit, and she ______ much junk food. Usually, she ______ tennis once a month, but now she ______ karate twice a week, too. I really need to do something like that. I ______ anything to stay healthy. :)

## 3 About you

Grammar and vocabulary | **Are these sentences true or false for you? Write *T* (true) or *F* (false). Then correct the false statements.**

1. *F* I'm drinking a lot of milk these days.
   *I'm not drinking a lot of milk these days. I'm drinking a lot of soda.*
2. ____ My best friend eats junk food every day.
   ______________________________
3. ____ I'm not taking any classes right now.
   ______________________________
4. ____ I sleep for five hours a night.
   ______________________________
5. ____ My friends have a lot of stress in their lives.
   ______________________________
6. ____ My family doesn't get any exercise at all.
   ______________________________

## 1 What's the matter?

Vocabulary **A** There are seven health problems in the puzzle. Find the other six. Look in these directions (→ ↓).

| | | | | | | | | | | | |
|---|---|---|---|---|---|---|---|---|---|---|---|
| A | T | O | O | T | H | A | C | H | E | W | A |
| B | C | K | F | M | U | U | O | E | R | F | L |
| S | O | R | E | T | H | R | O | A | T | D | L |
| R | U | I | V | D | E | I | H | D | U | J | E |
| V | G | J | P | L | A | R | U | P | L | A | F |
| E | H | C | S | H | E | A | D | A | C | H | E |
| S | I | O | T | B | J | W | L | S | A | N | V |
| O | H | L | F | O | V | A | O | U | B | D | E |
| B | E | A | L | L | E | R | G | I | E | S | R |
| G | A | N | G | D | C | K | S | W | N | C | H |
| S | T | O | M | A | C | H | A | C | H | E | I |
| R | M | R | L | T | N | F | R | G | C | S | R |

**B** Look at the picture. Write sentences with the words from part A.

1. *Joe has a fever.*
2. ______
3. ______
4. ______
5. ______
6. ______
7. ______

# 2 I feel sick.

Grammar and vocabulary **Look at the pictures. Write questions and answers.**

1. *What does Ann do when she has the flu?*
   When *Ann has the flu, she stays in bed*.
2. ______________________
   If ______________________.

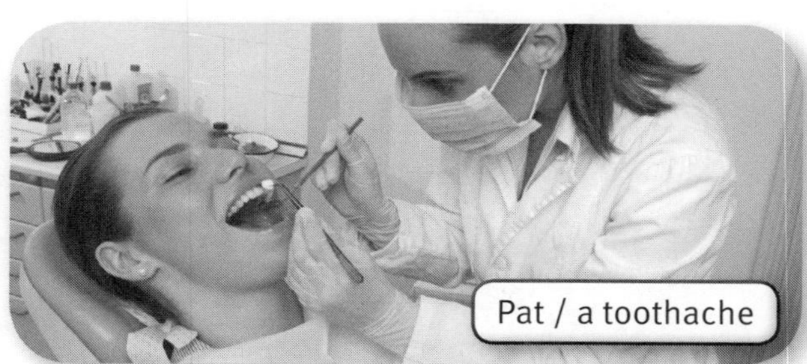


3. ______________________
   ____________ when ____________.
4. ______________________
   ____________ if ____________.

# 3 About you

Grammar and vocabulary **Write questions for a friend using *when* or *if*. Then answer your friend's questions.**

1. **You** *What do you do when you're sick?*
   (when / are sick)
   **Friend** When I'm sick, I stay home and watch movies all day. How about you?
   **You** ______________________
2. **You** ______________________
   (if / have a bad cough)
   **Friend** I usually take cough medicine if I have a bad cough. What do you do?
   **You** ______________________
3. **You** ______________________
   (if / get an upset stomach)
   **Friend** If I get an upset stomach, I drink water. I don't eat a lot. How about you?
   **You** ______________________
4. **You** ______________________
   (when / have a fever)
   **Friend** When I have a fever, I take aspirin and I don't go out. What about you?
   **You** ______________________

# Lesson C / Really? How come?

## 1 It's my allergies.

Conversation strategies | **Complete the conversation. Use the sentences in the box.**

| | |
|---|---|
| Are you serious? How come? I mean, why not? | Gosh, that's terrible! So, what are you studying? |
| ✓ Oh, no! That's too bad. Do you sneeze a lot? | Really? So how do you study when you don't feel good? |
| You're kidding! So you never take medicine? | |
| Headaches? Do you take anything? | |

Joan Gary, are you OK? Your eyes are all red.
Gary Oh, it's my allergies. I always feel this way in the spring.
Joan *Oh, no! That's too bad. Do you sneeze a lot?*
Gary Yeah. I sneeze all the time. And I get headaches, too.
Joan ______________________________
Gary Not really. Actually, I don't like to take medicine.
Joan ______________________________
Gary No. Never. And especially allergy medicine. If I take it, I can't study.
Joan ______________________________
Gary Well, you see, when I take medicine, I always fall asleep.
Joan ______________________________
Gary It's hard, but I have to try. Right now I'm studying for a big test next week.
Joan ______________________________
Gary I'm studying medicine!

## 2 You're kidding!

Conversation strategies | **Circle the best response to show surprise.**

1. My husband talks in his sleep.
   a. My husband does, too.
   (b.) Wow! What does he say?

2. I love getting up early on weekends.
   a. Do you get up early on weekdays, too?
   b. Are you serious? On weekends?

3. I take two or three naps every day.
   a. Gosh! Do you sleep OK at night?
   b. I know. I saw you fall asleep in class once!

4. I often drink hot chocolate if I can't sleep.
   a. Me too. I love hot chocolate at night.
   b. You're kidding! It keeps me awake.

5. My grandmother goes running six days a week.
   a. No way! How old is she?
   b. So she's really into exercise, huh?

6. I often dream about food.
   a. I do too. I always dream about ice cream.
   b. Really? Are you hungry when you go to bed?

7. I have three part-time jobs.
   a. Oh, wow! You work really hard.
   b. Do you often get tired?

8. If I can't sleep, I often listen to rock music.
   a. Gosh! I can't sleep with music on.
   b. Me too. I also listen to pop music.

## 3 No way!

Conversation strategies

**Write responses to show surprise. Then ask follow-up questions.**

1. A One of my friends cleans the house when he can't sleep.
   B *No way!* ______ *So does he go back to bed at all?*
2. A My best friend remembers all her dreams.
   B ______ ______
3. A I sometimes sleep at the office.
   B ______ ______
4. A Sometimes I can't sleep because my neighbors play loud music.
   B ______ ______
5. A My little brother has the same nightmare about once a month.
   B ______ ______
6. A My father sleepwalks every night.
   B ______ ______
7. A I never use an alarm clock.
   B ______ ______
8. A My sister goes running right after she eats dinner.
   B ______ ______

## 4 About you

Conversation strategies

**Answer the questions with your own information.**

1. Are you feeling sleepy right now? ______
2. How often do you take naps on weekdays? ______
3. Do you ever sleep in class or at work? ______
4. Are you sleeping well these days? ______
5. What do you do when you wake up at night? ______
6. Do you dream in color? ______

# Health advice

## 1 Understanding stress

Reading **A Read the leaflet. Which of these are signs of stress? Check (✓) the boxes.**

- [ ] You have health problems.
- [ ] You can't concentrate.
- [ ] You have a lot of energy.
- [ ] You are tired.
- [ ] You breathe slowly.
- [ ] You feel irritable.

### Common Questions About Stress

**Am I stressed?**

If you can't sleep well or can't concentrate, . . .
If you feel depressed or want to cry a lot, . . .
If you have a headache or an upset stomach, . . .
If you can't relax and you feel irritable, . . .
If you are extremely tired, . . .

. . . then it's possible you are stressed.

**Is stress bad for me?**

Occasional stress is common and not always bad for you. However, if you feel stressed for a long time, it can be serious. Stress can make you sick. It can also affect your memory or concentration, so it's hard to get your work done.

**What can I do?**

Fortunately, there's a lot you can do. Try some of these relaxation techniques. If you still feel stressed, then make an appointment to see your doctor.

### Relaxation Techniques

1. **Breathe** Take a breath, hold it for four seconds, and then breathe out very slowly. Feel your body relax.
2. **Exercise** Walk or exercise for just 30 minutes each day and feel better.

3. **Talk** Call a friend. Talk about your problems.
4. **Meditate** Close your eyes and focus on something calm. Feel relaxed.
5. **Pamper yourself** Take a hot bath, or have a massage.

6. **Do something you enjoy** Listen to music. Sing. Watch TV. Meet a friend for coffee.

*Department of Health – "Take care of yourself."*

**B Read the leaflet again. Then choose the correct words to complete the sentences.**

| | | a. | b. |
|---|---|---|---|
| 1. | When you're stressed, it's not easy to *relax*. | a. relax | b. cry |
| 2. | Stress ________ a lot of people. | a. affects | b. doesn't affect |
| 3. | Stress is ________ good for you. | a. sometimes | b. never |
| 4. | If you're very stressed, you often can't ________. | a. exercise | b. think |
| 5. | One good relaxation technique is to ________. | a. see a doctor | b. take a bath |

## 2 Healthy lifestyles

Writing **A** **Read these suggestions for a healthy lifestyle. Add commas where necessary.**

# Healthy Habits

BY DR. GOODMAN

Take yoga classes. When you practice yoga, you stay in shape and relax at the same time.

If you can't sleep drink a glass of warm milk.

Sing at home or in your car if you want to have a lot of energy.

When you listen to music choose relaxing music.

If you feel sad take a long walk. Exercise can help your mood.

Do something you love when life is stressful.

**B** **Choose one of the titles below and write a short article. Give three suggestions.**

**Sleep** **Food and Diet** **Exercise**

## Unit 3 Progress chart

| | What can you do? Mark the boxes.<br>✓ = I can . . . ? = I need to review how to . . . | To review, go back to these pages in the Student's Book. |
|---|---|---|
| Grammar | ☐ make statements with the simple present and present continuous. | 22 and 23 |
| | ☐ ask questions with the simple present and present continuous. | 22 and 23 |
| | ☐ use *if* and *when* in statements and questions. | 25 |
| Vocabulary | ☐ name at least 8 healthy habits. | 22 and 23 |
| | ☐ name at least 4 unhealthy habits. | 22 and 23 |
| | ☐ name at least 6 health problems. | 24 and 25 |
| Conversation strategies | ☐ keep a conversation going with comments and follow-up questions. | 26 and 27 |
| | ☐ use expressions like *Wow!* or *You're kidding!* to show surprise. | 27 |
| Writing | ☐ use commas in *if* and *when* clauses. | 29 |

# Celebrations

UNIT 4

## Lesson A Birthdays

### 1 What month is it?

Vocabulary **A Write the months in the correct order.**

1. *January*
2. ______
3. ______
4. ______
5. ______
6. ______
7. ______
8. ______
9. ______
10. ______
11. ______
12. ______

**B Complete the sentences with the correct numbers.**

1. January is the *first* month of the year.
2. March is the ______ month of the year.
3. June is the ______ month of the year.
4. July is the ______ month of the year.
5. October is the ______ month of the year.
6. December is the ______ month of the year.

### 2 When's her birthday?

Grammar and vocabulary **Look at the dates. Then write each person's birthday two ways.**

1. *Halle Berry's birthday is on August fourteenth.*
   *Her birthday is on the fourteenth of August.*
2. ______
3. ______
4. ______
5. ______
6. ______

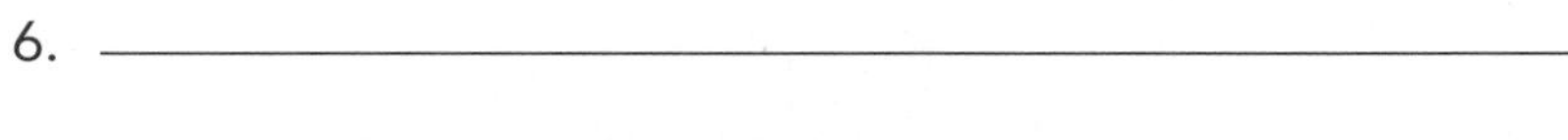

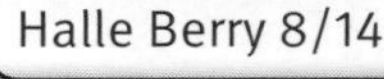

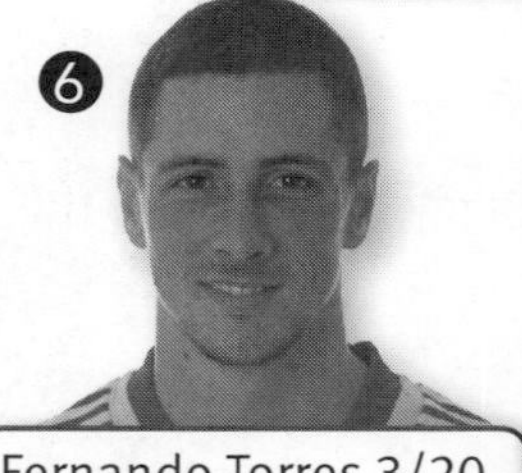

## 3 Future plans

Grammar | **Complete the conversations with the correct form of *be going to*.**

1. **Sam** What *are you going to do* (you / do) this weekend?
   **Diane** I ____________ (see) my grandmother. We ____________ (have) a birthday party for her.
   **Sam** That's nice. How ____________ (you / celebrate)? I mean, ____________ (it / be) a big party?
   **Diane** No, not really. We ____________ (not do) much. It ____________ (be) just the family. Mom ____________ (bake) her a cake. Then her friends ____________ (take) her dancing. She's a tango teacher.
   **Sam** Your grandmother's a tango teacher? Cool.

2. **Yumi** That was Jun on the phone. He can't take us to Sarah's party.
   **Kara** Oh, no. Why not?
   **Yumi** No car. His parents ____________ (go) away this weekend, and they ____________ (take) the car.
   **Kara** Huh. Where ____________ (they / go)? Well, anyway, ____________ Dan ____________ (be) there?
   **Yumi** Yeah, but he ____________ (not go) until after work.
   **Kara** Well, it looks like we ____________ (have to) walk. Wear comfortable shoes!

## 4 Happy birthday!

Grammar and vocabulary | **Complete the card. Put the words in order.**

Happy Birthday

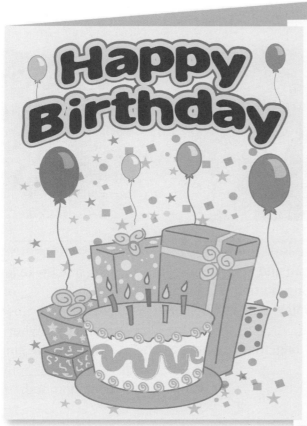

*Dear Kathleen,*

*Happy birthday! I'm sending you this card (sending / this / you / card / I'm) from Mexico. Hector and I are in Mexico City; we're visiting his parents. ____________ (us / all the sights / showing / 're / They ). His mother Beatriz is so nice. ____________ (some / I / her / jewelry / brought) from New York, and she wears it everywhere. ____________ (me / is / Beatriz / teaching / Spanish) and how to make Mexican food. She says ____________ (to / get / she / going / us / 's) a tamale pot to take home. Hector loves tamales, and ____________ (tamales / want to / him / make / I) on special occasions. We want to take his parents to a nice restaurant, but ____________ (dinner / can / them / we / buy / never). They never let us pay for anything!*

*Anyway, how about you? ____________ (I / Can / you / bring / anything) from Mexico for your birthday?*

*Ellen*

## 1 Good times

Vocabulary | **Look at the pictures. Write the special event. Then complete the descriptions with the expressions in the box.**

| | | |
|---|---|---|
| blow out (the) candle | go out for a romantic dinner | shout "Happy New Year" |
| exchange rings | go trick-or-treating | sing "Happy Birthday" |
| get a diploma | have a reception | ✓wear a cap and gown |
| give her chocolates | see the fireworks | wear costumes |

*graduation day*

1. Ana and her classmates have to *wear a cap and gown* . When they call her name, Ana's going to ____________ .

____________

2. The waiters ____________ when they bring out a cake. Erin's going to make a wish and ____________ .

____________

3. Allen and Carine decided to ____________ . After dinner, Allen's going to ____________ .

____________

4. Bruce and Sheila are at a big party on the beach. They wanted to ____________ . At midnight, they're going to ____________ .

____________

5. Ahmad and Keisha are getting married. During the wedding, they're going to ____________ . After the wedding, they're going to ____________ .

____________

6. John and Blake love to ____________ of their favorite comic-book characters. When they're ready, they're going to ____________ in the neighborhood.

## 2 A busy week

Grammar | **Read George's calendar. Write a sentence about each plan. Use the present continuous.**

| MAY | | | | | | |
|---|---|---|---|---|---|---|
| Sunday | Monday | Tuesday | Wednesday | Thursday | Friday | Saturday |
| 8<br>Mother's Day – have lunch with Mom | 9<br>**8:00** – Meet Ann for dinner | 10<br>Play tennis with Greg after work | 11<br>**8:00** – See a movie with Joe | 12<br>Work out with Dan before work | 13<br>**2:00** – Give a speech at Keith and Karen's wedding | 14<br>**5:00** – Go to Jennifer's graduation party |

1. *On May eighth, George is having lunch with his mother.*
2. ______________________
3. ______________________
4. ______________________
5. ______________________
6. ______________________
7. ______________________

## 3 What's going to happen?

Grammar | **Write a prediction about each picture. Use *be going to*. Some are negative.**

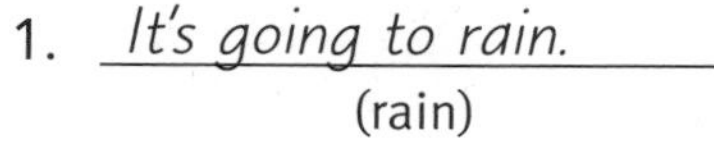

1. *It's going to rain.*
(rain)

2. ______________________
(go trick-or-treating)

3. ______________________
(give / flowers)

4. ______________________
(see / fireworks)

5. ______________________
(get a diploma)

6. ______________________
(be sunny)

# Lesson C / It depends.

##  "Vague" expressions

Conversation strategies

**Rewrite the underlined words, if possible, using vague expressions like *and everything, and stuff (like that)*, or *and things (like that)*. You can't rewrite some of them.**

1. **Maya** Let's do something different this year for New Year's. Like take a vacation.

   **Jake** OK. We work hard, and I think we really need a break.

   **Maya** Yes, I'd like to go away on vacation and lie on a beach and read ~~and relax and sleep~~ *and stuff*.

   **Jake** Yeah, and then in the evenings we can have some nice romantic dinners with candles and music and nice food.

   **Maya** Or we can go to movies and concerts and listen to local bands and singers.

   **Jake** Could you give me my tablet? We can look online, and I'm sure we can find a nice place to go.

   **Maya** Just one thing. Who's going to tell everyone, especially your parents, that we're not going to be at the family party this year?

2. **Sonia** Hey, there's a Rodeo Days festival today and tomorrow. What is it exactly?

   **Pete** Well, every February they have this festival, and all the kids dress up in cowboy costumes with cowboy boots and hats and scarves. And they ride horses, and there's a parade and competitions and exhibits. So what do you think? Do you want to go?

   **Sonia** Maybe. I don't know, I'm not big on rodeos and cowboys and horses.

   **Pete** Well, it's really kind of fun. And people sell jewelry and T-shirts and belts and boots and hats.

   **Sonia** Well, that sounds fun.

   **Pete** And they have cowboy food like beans and steak and other kinds of cowboy food.

   **Sonia** Oh, OK. So let's go – maybe this afternoon?

## 2 About you

Conversation strategies

**Answer the questions with the responses in the box. Use each response only once. Then add more information.**

✓I don't know. | I'm not sure. | It depends. | Maybe.

1. Are you going to celebrate your birthday with a party and everything?

   *I don't know. My girlfriend usually surprises me on my birthday.*

2. What do you want to do this weekend?

   ______

3. Are you going to send your mother some flowers on her birthday?

   ______

4. Do you want to go see the fireworks tonight?

   ______

## 3 Scrambled conversation

Conversation strategies

**Number the lines of the conversation in the correct order.**

- ☐ But you can also shop for cool Chinese gifts and things.
- ☐ *1* Would you like to go to a Chinese festival?
- ☐ Well, maybe. What do people do?
- ☐ There's going to be free food? Great, I'd love to go.
- ☐ Well, I don't know. I'm not big on dances and stuff like that.
- ☐ Well, at least the food is great, and it's free.
- ☐ Uh, maybe, but I don't have money for shopping right now.
- ☐ It's for Chinese New Year.
- ☐ Lots of things, like lion dances, fireworks, and everything!
- ☐ I'm not sure. What kind of festival is it exactly?

## 1 Celebrating mothers

Reading | **A Read the article. Then add the correct heading to each paragraph.**

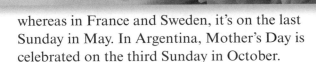

| | |
|---|---|
| History of the holiday | When is Mother's Day? |
| Ideas for Mother's Day | ✓Why people celebrate Mother's Day |
| Traditional ways to celebrate | |

# *Mother's Day*

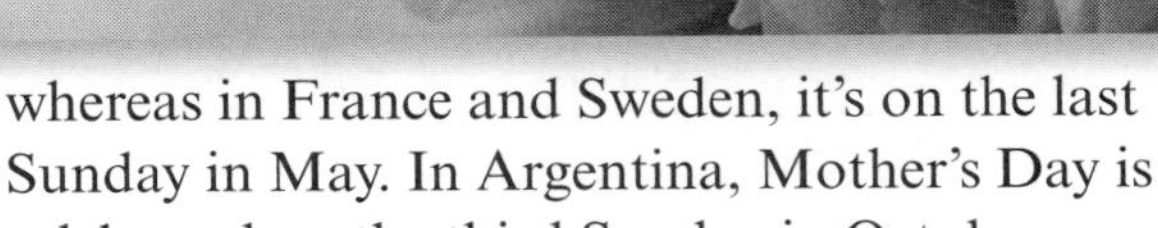

*Why people celebrate Mother's Day*

In many countries, there is a special day of the year when children of all ages celebrate their mothers. On this day – Mother's Day – children tell their mothers that they love them, and thank them for their love and care.

____________________

Mother's Day is not a new celebration. Historians say that it started as a spring festival in ancient Greece. The modern festival of Mother's Day probably comes from England in the 1600s, when people had a day off from their jobs to visit their mothers on a day they called "Mothering Sunday." They took small gifts and a special cake called "simnel cake." In the United States, Mother's Day became an official holiday in 1914.

____________________

People in different countries celebrate Mother's Day on different days. In Spain and Portugal, Mother's Day is the first Sunday in May. In Australia, Brazil, Italy, Japan, Turkey, and the United States, it's on the second Sunday in May, whereas in France and Sweden, it's on the last Sunday in May. In Argentina, Mother's Day is celebrated on the third Sunday in October.

____________________

Although many countries celebrate Mother's Day at different times of the year, the holidays have one purpose in common – to show love and appreciation for mothers. For example, on Mother's Day morning, some children give their mothers gifts they made especially for this holiday.

____________________

What are you going to do next Mother's Day? Maybe you can use some of these ideas to make your mother feel special.

- *Make or buy your mother a beautiful Mother's Day card*
- *Write her a letter telling her why you appreciate her*
- *Make her a special meal or bake a cake*
- *Plant a flower or tree somewhere she can see it*

**B Read the article again. Answer the questions.**

1. Where did the idea of Mother's Day come from originally? *It came from ancient Greece.*
2. Which country started the tradition of giving presents on Mother's Day? __________
3. What was Mother's Day called in England? __________
4. When do Brazil and Japan celebrate Mother's Day? __________
5. What do you do on Mother's Day? __________

## 2 Making plans

Writing **A** Start and end these notes to different people.

**An email to a friend**

New Message
To: steve_P@cup.com
Subject: MY PARTY

*Hi Steve,*

I'm having a party on Saturday night. Everybody's going to be there. Hope you can make it.

*See you then.*

**A note to your neighbor**

______

*I'm having a party on Friday. We're going to have a band. I hope it's not too noisy. Please join us.*

______

**An email to your teacher**

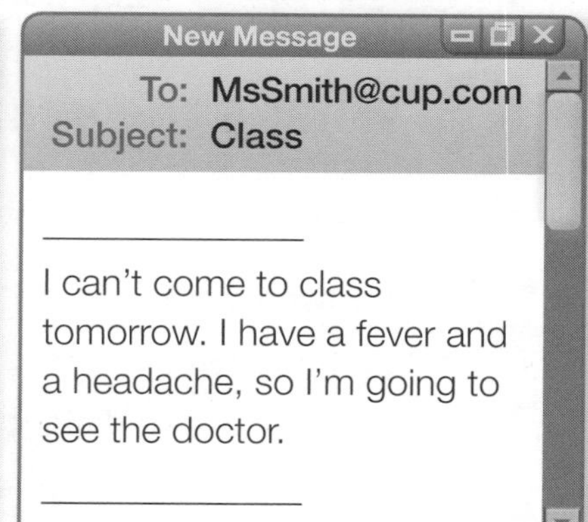

New Message
To: MsSmith@cup.com
Subject: Class

______

I can't come to class tomorrow. I have a fever and a headache, so I'm going to see the doctor.

______

**B** Write to these people about a special celebration.

**An email to a teacher**

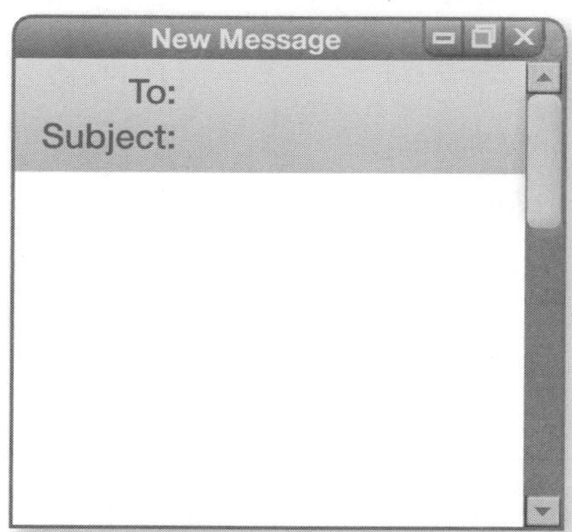

New Message
To:
Subject:

**A note to a friend**

**An email to your grandparents**

New Message
To:
Subject:

## Unit 4 Progress chart

| | What can you do? Mark the boxes.<br>✓ = I can . . . ? = I need to review how to . . . | To review, go back to these pages in the Student's Book. |
|---|---|---|
| Grammar | ☐ use *be going to* for the future.<br>☐ use indirect objects and indirect object pronouns.<br>☐ use the present continuous for specific future plans. | 35, 36, and 37<br>34 and 35<br>37 |
| Vocabulary | ☐ say dates with the months of the year and ordinal numbers.<br>☐ describe things people do on holidays and special days. | 34<br>34 |
| Conversation strategies | ☐ use "vague" expressions like *and everything* and *and things*.<br>☐ use "vague" responses like *I don't know* and *Maybe*. | 38 and 39<br>39 |
| Writing | ☐ start and end invitations, emails, and personal notes. | 41 |

# Growing up

UNIT 5

## Lesson A / Childhood

### 1 What's the year?

Vocabulary | **Write the years in numbers or words.**

1. twenty ten *2010*
2. nineteen oh-four ________
3. two thousand eight ________
4. nineteen seventy-seven ________
5. 1982 *nineteen eighty-two*
6. 2006 ________
7. 2013 ________
8. 1998 ________

### 2 Talking about the past

Grammar | **Complete the conversations with *was*, *wasn't*, *were*, *weren't*, *did*, or *didn't*.**

1\.
**Rick** So, Dina, *did* you grow up here in Miami?
**Dina** Yes, I ________ , but we ________ born here. My sister and I ________ born in Puerto Rico, and we moved here when we ________ kids.
**Rick** So, ________ you study English when you ________ in school in Puerto Rico?
**Dina** Yes, we ________ – for a few years – but we ________ really learn English until we came here.
**Rick** Wow! And now you speak English better than I do – and I ________ born here!

LIBRARY

2\.
**Thomas** When *were* you born, Grandma?
**Grandma** I ________ born in 1934.
**Thomas** Really? ________ you born here in Los Angeles?
**Grandma** No, I ________ . Your grandfather and I ________ both born in China.
**Thomas** So when ________ you come to the U.S.?
**Grandma** My family ________ move here until I ________ 13 years old.
**Thomas** Really? So ________ you sad to leave all your friends and family in China?
**Grandma** Yes, we ________ . But we ________ sad for long. We soon made friends and everything.
**Thomas** That's good. When ________ Grandpa born?
**Grandma** He ________ born in 1933, but he says he ________ really born until 1952.
**Thomas** Why does he say that?
**Grandma** Because that's when he met *me*!

## 3 A life story

Grammar **Complete the story with the words in the box. You can use some words more than once.**

| ✓ago | for | from | in | last | long | then | to | until | when |
|---|---|---|---|---|---|---|---|---|---|

This is a picture of my best friend, Mi-young. I took it a few years *ago* . Mi-young and I met ________ 1994. We were very young ________ we became friends. Mi-young is a very interesting person. She was born in Busan, South Korea, ________ 1990. Her family moved to the U.S. ________ she was three years old. They lived in Chicago ________ Mi-young was 15. ________ they moved to New York City. I cried ________ a long time after they moved.

Mi-young didn't live in New York ________ because she came back to Chicago for college ________ she was 18. We were roommates at the University of Chicago ________ four years – ________ 2008 ________ 2012. We graduated and shared an apartment ________ a few months. ________ she got a great job in Phoenix, Arizona, and moved there. I really missed her, but guess what? ________ month she called and said there's a perfect job for me at her company. So I'm going there ________ October for an interview, and I can't wait!

## 4 About you

Grammar and vocabulary **Write questions using the prompts given. Then answer the questions with your own information.**

1. When / you born ? *When were you born?*
2. Where / your parents born ? ________
3. Where / you grow up ? ________
4. Who / your best friend five years ago ? ________
5. you / ever move when you were a child ? ________
6. you / play outside a lot when you were little ? ________
7. How old / you when you started school ? ________

# 1 What's the subject?

Vocabulary **A Cross out the word that doesn't belong. Then write the general category of the subjects.**

| | | | | |
|---|---|---|---|---|
| 1. history | ~~chemistry~~ | economics | geography | *social studies* |
| 2. gymnastics | dance | art | track | ________ |
| 3. geometry | computer studies | algebra | calculus | ________ |
| 4. literature | biology | chemistry | physics | ________ |
| 5. choir | band | drama | orchestra | ________ |

**B Complete the crossword puzzle.**

| | | | | | | | | | | |
|---|---|---|---|---|---|---|---|---|---|---|
| 1. *a* | *l* | 2. *g* | *e* | *b* | *r* | 3. *a* | ■ | ■ | ■ | ■ |
| ■ | ■ | | ■ | ■ | ■ | | ■ | 4. | ■ | 5. |
| ■ | ■ | | ■ | 6. | ■ | | ■ | | ■ | |
| ■ | ■ | | ■ | | ■ | ■ | ■ | | ■ | |
| ■ | 7. | | | | | ■ | ■ | | ■ | |
| ■ | ■ | | ■ | | ■ | 8. | | | | |
| ■ | ■ | | ■ | | ■ | ■ | ■ | | ■ | |
| ■ | ■ | 9. | | | | | | | ■ | |
| ■ | ■ | | ■ | | ■ | ■ | ■ | ■ | ■ | |
| ■ | ■ | ■ | ■ | | ■ | ■ | ■ | ■ | ■ | |
| 10. | | | | | ■ | ■ | ■ | ■ | ■ | |

**Across**

1. This is one subject in math.
7. Students run short and long distances in this P.E. class.
8. Students learn to sing in this music class.
9. In this subject, students study about people and events from a long time ago.
10. Students learn to be actors when they study this subject.

**Down**

2. In this class, students study countries of the world and natural features, populations, and climate.
3. Students draw and paint in this class.
4. This subject is a science. Students learn about plant and animal life.
5. In this subject, teachers ask students to read novels, stories, and poems.
6. In this class, students play classical music on instruments.

## 2 How did we do?

Grammar | **A Write the determiners in order in the chart below.**

a few ✓all a lot of most none of some

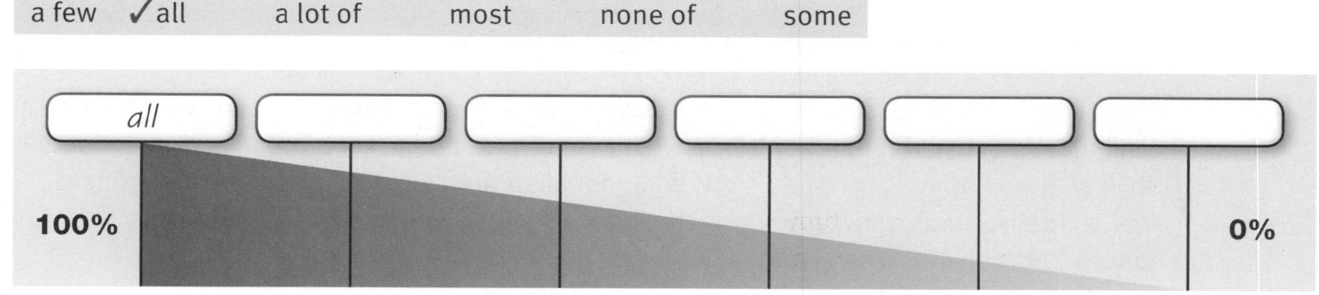


**B Read the test results. Then complete the sentences with the words in the box and add *of* where necessary. Some expressions are used more than once.**

| | A | B | C | D | E |
|---|---|---|---|---|---|
| 1 | | **Chemistry** | **English** | **Geography** | **Geometry** |
| 2 | **Passed** | 55% | 100% | 90% | 15% |
| 3 | **Failed** | 45% | 0% | 10% | 85% |

A few All A lot Most None Some

1. ___Some___ students in the class passed chemistry. ________ them failed chemistry.
2. ________ the students passed English. ________ the students failed it.
3. ________ the students passed geography. ________ students failed it.
4. ________ students passed geometry. ________ them failed it.

## 3 About you

Grammar and vocabulary | **Answer the questions with your own information. If you are still in high school, write about last year.**

**When you were in high school, what was a subject . . .**

1. most of your friends liked? *Most of my friends liked P.E.*
2. all of the students had to study? ________
3. a lot of students hated? ________
4. some of your classmates loved? ________
5. no students ever failed? ________
6. a few students were always really good at? ________
7. none of your classmates liked? ________
8. a lot of students got good grades in? ________
9. some students dropped? ________

# Lesson C Well, actually, . . .

## Correcting things you say

Conversation strategies **Complete the conversations with the sentences in the box.**

| | |
|---|---|
| Actually, no, it was 2009. | Actually, I guess I spent some weekends with my grandparents. |
| Well, at least most of them didn't. | Well, actually, we had a few problems. My dad lost his job. |
| No, wait. I was nine. | ✓Well, not all of them. Josie speaks three languages. |
| Well, actually, it was dark brown. | No, wait. . . . Her name was Mrs. Santos. |
| Actually, no, I was 18 when I quit. | |

1. A All my friends are bilingual. They all speak two languages.
   *Well, not all of them. Josie speaks three languages.*
   B That's amazing!
2. A My best friend and I had sleepovers every weekend when we were kids.
   ____________________
   B That sounds like fun.
3. A We moved to Rio de Janeiro when I was ten.
   ____________________
   B So you were pretty young.
4. A I was on a swimming team until I was 16.
   ____________________
   B That's the reason you swim so well.
5. A My brother and I had a perfect childhood.
   ____________________
   B Really? But you were generally pretty happy, right?
6. A My cousin lived with us for a year – in 2010, I think.
   ____________________
   B That was your cousin Alice, right?
7. A My favorite teacher in elementary school was Mrs. Santana.
   ____________________
   B Oh, yeah? My favorite teacher was Mr. Stiller.
8. A When I was little, none of my friends had pets.
   ____________________
   B But you had a dog, right?
9. A I had black hair when I was born.
   ____________________
   B Really? I was born with no hair at all!

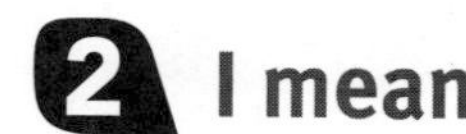

## I mean

Conversation strategies

**Complete the questions using *I mean* to correct the underlined words. Then answer the questions.**

1. When you were a child, what was the name of your first professor, *I mean, teacher* ?
   ______________________________
2. Were you six or seven when you started high school, ______________ ?
   ______________________________
3. In elementary school, did you have lunch in the school gym, ______________ ?
   ______________________________
4. When you were young, what was your favorite sport, ______________ ?
   Did you like checkers? ______________________________
5. When you were young, did you play any music, ______________ , like the piano?
   ______________________________

## 3 About you

Conversation strategies

**Complete these sentences so they are true for you.**

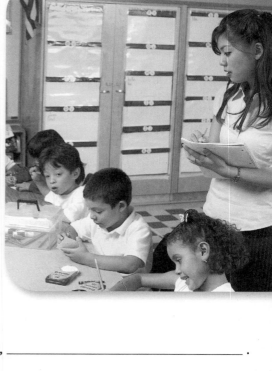

1. I started school when I was three. Actually, no,
   *when I was five* .
2. The name of my elementary school was Park Elementary.
   No, wait. . . . ______________________________ .
3. My first teacher's name was Miss Parker, I mean,
   ______________________________ .
4. I got good grades in every subject. Well, ______________
   ______________________________ .
5. Most of my childhood friends liked classical music. Well,
   no, ______________________________ .
6. When I was a child, my favorite holiday was Halloween, I
   mean, ______________________________ .
7. I remember all my classmates in kindergarten. Well, actually, ______________________________ .
8. A lot of my friends did gymnastics or played sports after school.
   No, wait. . . . ______________________________ .
9. We always had pizza for school lunch.
   Well, actually, ______________________________ .

## 1 Small-town story

Reading | **A Read the story of Yolanda's life. Then number the pictures in the correct order.**

☐ 

☐ 

☐ 

☐ 

### Interview: A happy childhood by Kathy Montaño

*Kathy Montaño grew up in the small town of Bagdad, Arizona. She interviewed several Mexican Americans in Bagdad about their childhood. This is the story of Yolanda Sandoval.*

"My name is Yolanda Sandoval. I was born in Cananea, Mexico, on June 13, 1922. My parents brought me to Bagdad when I was six months old. My father's name was Francisco Sandoval, and my mother's name was Cecilia Bernal.

I was their first child. I have four younger brothers. My mother gave Rafael, my third brother, her name as a middle name. Apart from Rafael, no one had a middle name. My mother was very gentle and patient.

My father was very kind but strict. He worked in a mine. He didn't talk much about his work, maybe because he didn't like it. My mother didn't go out to work. She stayed home to take care of us.

My mother always did special things for our birthdays. One year she gave me a purple party. Everything was purple, even the drinks! She also made me a purple dress. That was the best party I ever had. I invited all my friends – except for Bobby. I was angry with him at the time. My mother died when I was 16. I still miss her.

My brothers and I loved the movies. We thought they were wonderful. A man named Angel Ruiz showed old cowboy movies at the local theater, and we went to all of them. He charged five cents for a movie. Sometimes we didn't have the five cents, but he let us see the movie anyway.

I loved school. I had to study English for four years, science for two (I took chemistry and biology), and a foreign language for two years. I took Spanish, of course! Spanish was easy for me, so I got good grades. I also studied U.S. history, home economics, and physical education. I was a good student."

**B Read Yolanda's story again. Then complete the sentences.**

1. Kathy Montaño interviewed several people in her town about *their childhood*.
2. Yolanda Sandoval came to Bagdad when she ______________________.
3. Yolanda's father didn't talk much about his work because ______________________.
4. On Yolanda's birthday one year, her mother gave her ______________________.
5. At the local movie theater, Yolanda and her brothers saw ______________________.
6. Yolanda studied English for ______________________.

## 2 When I was a teenager

Writing **A Answer these questions about your first year in high school. If you are still in high school, talk about last year. Use *except (for)* or *apart from*.**

1. Did you like your teachers?
   *I liked all my teachers except for my history teacher, Mr. Crown.*
2. Did you enjoy all your subjects?
   ______________________________
3. Did you get along with all your classmates?
   ______________________________
4. Did you and your best friend do a lot of things together?
   ______________________________

**B Write about some of your favorite activities when you were a teenager.**

*When I was a teenager, I lived in*
*My friends and I loved to*

## Unit 5 Progress chart

| | What can you do? Mark the boxes.<br>✓ = I can . . . ? = I need to review how to . . . | To review, go back to these pages in the Student's Book. |
|---|---|---|
| Grammar | ☐ make statements and ask questions with the simple past and past of *be*. | 44 and 45 |
| | ☐ talk about the past using time expressions. | 44 and 45 |
| | ☐ use determiners: *all (of)*, *most (of)*, *a lot of*, *some (of)*, *a few (of)*, *no*, *none of*. | 46 and 47 |
| Vocabulary | ☐ say years. | 45 |
| | ☐ name at least 12 school subjects. | 47 |
| | ☐ name at least 5 general subject categories. | 47 |
| Conversation strategies | ☐ correct things I say with expressions like *Actually* and *No, wait*. | 48 and 49 |
| | ☐ use *I mean* to correct myself. | 49 |
| Writing | ☐ use *except (for)* and *apart from* to link ideas. | 51 |

# Around town

UNIT 6

## Lesson A Finding places

### Where is it?

Grammar and vocabulary **Look at the map. Write two answers for each question.**



1. Where's the bookstore? *It's on Pine Street, between the bank and the drugstore.*
   *It's across the street from the gas station.*
2. Where are the public restrooms? ______________________
3. Where's the parking lot? ______________________
4. Where are the ATMs? ______________________
5. Where's the gas station? ______________________
6. Where's the drugstore? ______________________

## 2 Looking for places

Grammar | **Write questions. Then complete the answers with *there's one*, *there are some*, *there isn't one*, or *there aren't any*.**

1. A *Is there a drugstore around here?*
   (drugstore around here ?)
   B Yes, *there's one* on the corner of Pine Street and Second Avenue.
2. A ______________________
   (parking lot near here ?)
   B ______________ on Oak Street, behind the bookstore.
3. A ______________________
   (ATMs anywhere ?)
   B ______________ over there, across from the gas station.
4. A ______________________
   (museum in this town ?)
   B No, sorry, ______________ .
5. A ______________________
   (outdoor cafés near here ?)
   B No, ______________ outdoor cafés near here, but there are some restaurants inside the department store on Pine Street.
6. A ______________________
   (public restrooms around here ?)
   B Yeah, sure, ______________ on Third Avenue.

## 3 About you

Grammar and vocabulary | **Write questions. Then answer the questions about your neighborhood.**

1. A (a good coffee shop) *Is there a good coffee shop in this neighborhood?*
   B *Yes, there is. There's Emily's on the corner of Center Avenue and First Street.*
2. A (a big department store) ______________________
   B ______________________
3. A (any unusual stores) ______________________
   B ______________________
4. A (a convenience store) ______________________
   B ______________________
5. A (any cheap restaurants) ______________________
   B ______________________
6. A (any ATMs) ______________________
   B ______________________

## 1 Places in town

Vocabulary | **Complete the sentences with the places in the box.**

| | | | | |
|---|---|---|---|---|
| aquarium | museum | running path | stadium | Visitor's Center |
| ✓hotel | parking garage | skateboard ramp | theater | water park |

**You can . . .**

1. sleep at a *hotel* .
2. see sea animals at an ____________ .
3. go jogging on a ____________ .
4. go skateboarding on a ____________ .
5. see a play at a ____________ .
6. see art and interesting exhibits at a ____________ .
7. ask for information at a ____________ .
8. leave your car at a ____________ .
9. watch a baseball game at a ____________ .
10. swim in an outdoor pool at a ____________ .

## 2 Where am I going?

Vocabulary | **Some people are at the Sea View Hotel. Where do they want to go? Look at the map. Complete the conversations with the names of the places.**

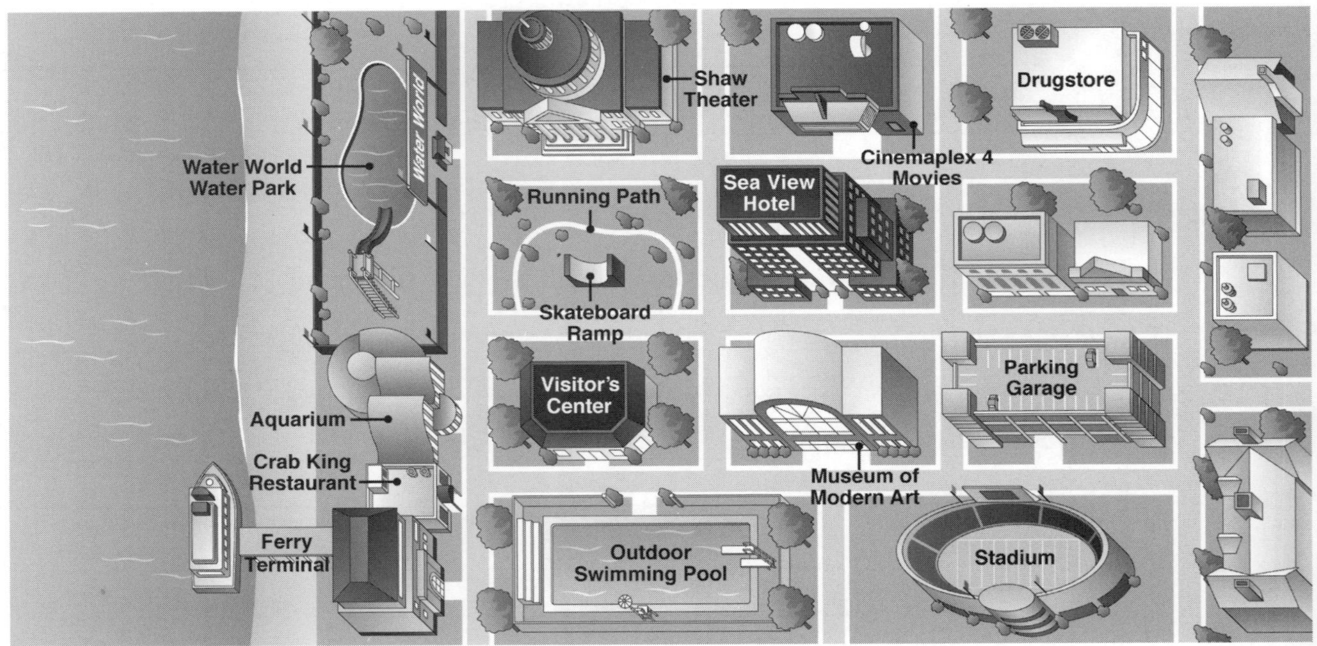


1. A Can you tell me how to get to the ____________ ?
   B Sure. When you leave the hotel, turn right. It's on the next block. It's there on your right.
2. A Can you tell me how to get to the ____________ ?
   B Yes. Go out of the hotel and turn left. Turn left again at the corner, go one block, and turn right. It's on your left.
3. A Can you help me? I'd like to go to the ____________ .
   B Yes. Turn right out of the hotel. Go straight for another block and make a left. Walk two blocks. It's on your right, next to the restaurant.

## 3 Directions, directions

Grammar and vocabulary **Rewrite the sentences to make requests. Then look at the map on page 44 and write directions.**

1. You're at the Visitor's Center. "Tell me how to get to the theater." (Could)
   A *Could you tell me how to get to the theater?*
   B *Sure. Turn right. Then take the first right. Walk straight ahead for two blocks. The theater is going to be there across the street on your right.*

2. You're at the aquarium. "Give me directions to the hotel." (Could)
   A ____________________
   B ____________________

3. You're at the aquarium. "Tell me how to get to the drugstore." (Can)
   A ____________________
   B ____________________

4. You're at the pool. "How do I get to the stadium?" (Can)
   A ____________________
   B ____________________

5. You're at the skateboard ramp. "Give me directions to the ferry terminal." (Could)
   A ____________________
   B ____________________

6. You're at the theater. "Tell me how to get to the parking garage." (Can)
   A ____________________
   B ____________________

## 4 About you

Grammar and vocabulary **Complete the offers and requests using *Can* or *Could*. Then answer the questions with true information about the neighborhood you are in now.**

1. A ____________________ recommend a nice restaurant around here?
   B ____________________

2. A Excuse me. I need some help. ____________________ help me?
   B Sure. How ____________________?
   A ____________________ get to the nearest hotel?
   B ____________________

3. A ____________________ directions to a park or a place to go running?
   B ____________________

## 1 Checking information

Conversation strategies | **Complete the conversations. Check the information.**

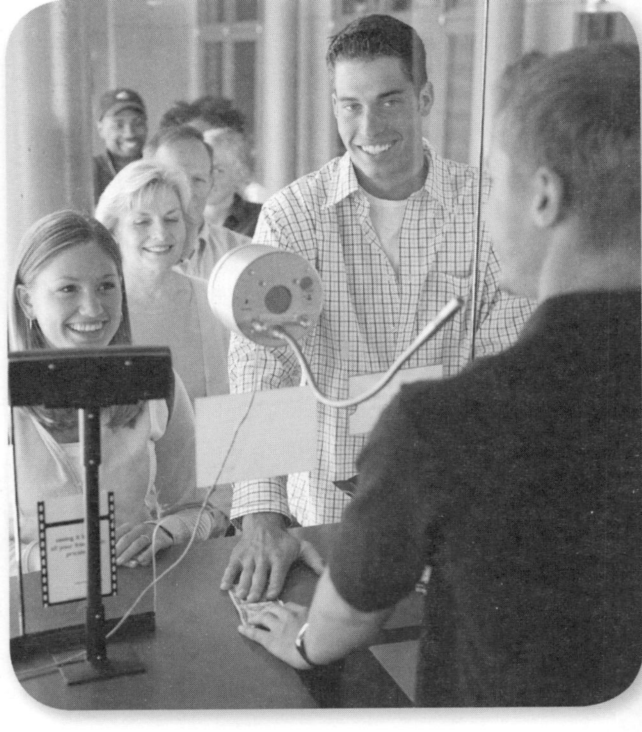

1. A Hi. Where to?
   B I'm going to 830 Center Street.
   A *I'm sorry? Did you say 813 Center Street?*
   B No, 830. That's on the corner of Center and Main – on the left side of the street.
   A ______________________________
   ______________________________
   B Yes, the left side.

2. A Could you tell me how to get to Atlantic Bank?
   B ______________________________
   A Yes. Do you know it?
   B I think so. Go straight ahead for three blocks and turn left. It's on the right.
   A ______________________________
   B No. Not on the left. It's on the right.

3. A Can I help you?
   B Yes, please. What time does the next show start?
   A At 7:15.
   B ______________________________
   A 7:15.
   B And what time does it end?
   A It ends at 9:05.
   B ______________________________
   A Yes, that's right.

4. A Can you give me directions to a pet store?
   B ______________________________
   A No, not a bookstore – a pet store. I want to buy some new fish for my aquarium.
   B Oh. Let me think. I think there's a pet store at Bay Street Mall.
   A ______________________________
   B Bay Street Mall. It's about half an hour from here.

## 2 I'm sorry?

Conversation strategies

**Complete the "echo" questions with the words in the box. Use each one only once. There are two extra.**

| how much | what | what kind | what time | when | where |
|---|---|---|---|---|---|

1. A A new deli opened right across the street from us.
   B I'm sorry, a new ________ opened?
   A A new deli. Let's try it. Then you don't need to cook!
2. A My brother spent almost five hundred dollars on theater tickets for his family.
   B Sorry? He spent ________ ?
   A Almost five hundred dollars. I hope it's a good show!
3. A I really want to leave at 6:00.
   B Sorry? You want to leave at ________ ?
   A At 6:00. Oh, it's already ten after. We're late!
4. A Did you remember? We're going to the aquarium today.
   B I'm sorry? We're going ________ ?
   A To the aquarium. Did you forget?

## 3 Questions, questions

Conversation strategies

**Complete the conversations with "echo" questions.**

1. A Do you have your wallet? The tickets are 60 dollars each.
   B They cost *how much?*
   A Sixty dollars each. Hurry. The show starts in 15 minutes. At 3:00.
   B At ____________ ?
   A At three. Hurry! It's going to be fun. There are going to be acrobats and things.
   B There are going to be ____________ ?
   Um, maybe we should just go to a movie instead!
2. A Let's go to the park today. There's a new bike path.
   B A new ____________ ?
   A A bike path. We can go cycling. And then we can go to Primm's.
   B We can go ____________ ?
   A Primm's. It's an ice cream place near the park. It sells really good pistachio ice cream.
   B Um, OK. But wait, it sells ____________ of ice cream?

# Lesson D Exploring the city

## 1 Life down under

Reading **A Read the article about Coober Pedy. Check (✓) the items the article talks about.**

- [ ] an amusement park
- [ ] an underground hotel
- [ ] a rock and roll museum
- [ ] a place that looks like the moon
- [ ] a drive-in movie theater
- [ ] an opal mine

Coober Pedy

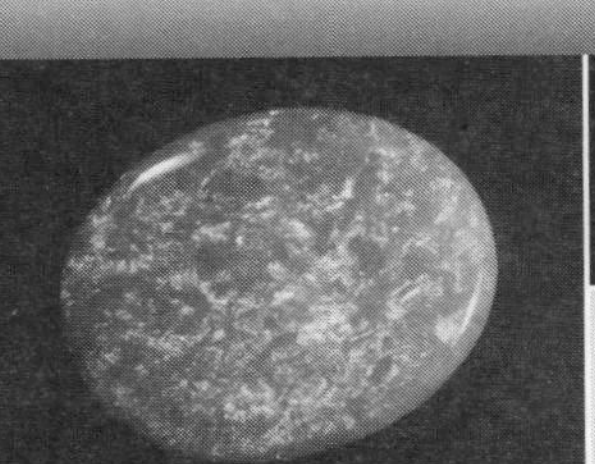

# COOBER PEDY
## —THE OPAL CAPITAL OF THE WORLD

Welcome to the desert town of Coober Pedy in the outback of Australia. The name Coober Pedy comes from the Aboriginal words *kupa piti*, which mean "white man in a hole." We hope you'll come visit.

Explorers first found opals in this area on February 1, 1915. In 1946, an Aboriginal woman named Tottie Bryant dug out a large and valuable opal. After that, a lot of people came to Coober Pedy to mine opals.

During the 1960s, many European immigrants came to work here, and Coober Pedy quickly became a large modern town. Today, Coober Pedy is the world's main source of high-quality opals and a unique tourist spot.

It's so hot in Coober Pedy that a lot of people live underground! There are many underground homes, as well as underground hotels, museums, opal shops, art galleries, and, of course, opal mines.

Here are some places to visit during your stay.

**Umoona Opal Mine & Museum** is a unique underground museum about the history of the town. It includes a model underground home and a small opal mine. Some of the world's finest opals are on display here.

**The Moon Plain** is a large rocky area unlike anywhere else. It looks like the moon – or another planet! It was the set for many movies, including *Mad Max Beyond Thunderdome, The Adventures of Priscilla, Queen of the Desert,* and *The Red Planet*. It is about 15 kilometers northeast of Coober Pedy.

**Coober Pedy Drive-In** is an open-air movie theater. You can see a movie there every other Saturday night.

**B Read the article again. Then match the two parts of each sentence.**

1. The name Coober Pedy means _d_
2. Tottie Bryant found ____
3. Coober Pedy became a modern mining town when ____
4. Right now, Coober Pedy is the world's main source ____
5. As a tourist place, Coober Pedy is famous for ____
6. The Moon Plain was ____

a. the set for many movies.
b. a very big and valuable opal.
c. its underground homes, museums, stores, and mines.
✓d. "white man in a hole."
e. immigrants came to work in the mines.
f. of high-quality opals.

## 2 Walking guide

Writing **A Read this New Orleans walking tour. Look at the map and fill in the missing words.**

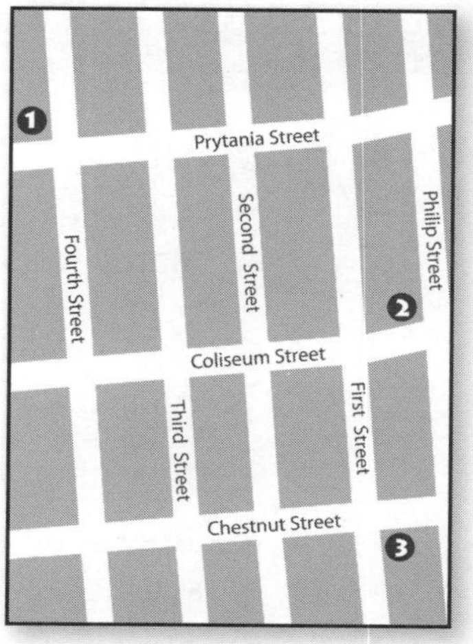

❶ This is the Garden District Book Shop. Anne Rice, a famous author from New Orleans, calls this her favorite bookstore.

❷ Take Prytania Street ___*four*___ blocks to Philip Street. Turn _________ on Philip Street. Take Philip Street one _________ to Coliseum Street. _________ a right on Coliseum Street. The homes on the _________ are called the Seven Sisters. A man wanted his seven daughters to live close to him. He built these seven houses for them as wedding gifts.

❸ Go _________ on Coliseum Street and walk to the end of the block. _________ left on First Street. Go _________ for one block. It's right there, on the _________ . This is the Brevard-Mahat-Rice House, where Anne Rice lives and works.



**B Think of two tourist attractions in your town or city. Write directions from one to the other.**

*Start at*

## Unit 6 Progress chart

| What can you do? Mark the boxes.<br>✓ = I can . . . ? = I need to review how to . . . | To review, go back to these pages in the Student's Book. |
|---|---|
| **Grammar** | |
| ☐ use *Is there?* and *Are there?* to ask about places in a town. | 54 and 55 |
| ☐ use *across from*, *behind*, *between*, etc., to describe location. | 55 |
| ☐ make offers and requests with *Can* and *Could*. | 56 and 57 |
| **Vocabulary** | |
| ☐ name at least 15 places in a city or town. | 54, 55, and 56 |
| **Conversation strategies** | |
| ☐ check information by repeating key words and using "checking" expressions. | 58 and 59 |
| ☐ ask "echo" questions to check information. | 59 |
| **Writing** | |
| ☐ write a guide giving directions. | 61 |

# Going away

UNIT 7

## Lesson A Getting ready

### 1 What are they going to do?

Grammar and vocabulary

**A Match the sentences.**

1. My friends are planning a trip to Ecuador. _d_
2. They're going to call a hotel near the airport. _____
3. They have to go to the bank. _____
4. They bought a guidebook. _____
5. They need to do some research. _____
6. They're going to the drugstore. _____

a. They wanted to learn more about the country.
b. They want to buy some travel-size toiletries.
c. They need to change some money.
✓d. They want to learn Spanish.
e. They want to find cheap flights.
f. They want to make a reservation for one night.

**B Combine the sentences. Write one sentence for each pair of sentences in part A.**

1. _My friends are going to go to Ecuador to learn Spanish._
2. ______________________________
3. ______________________________
4. ______________________________
5. ______________________________
6. ______________________________

## 2 Reasons for getting away

Grammar | **Imagine you are going to Australia for a vacation. Write sentences using the cues given.**

1. We want to *go to the Great Barrier Reef to learn to dive* .
   (go to the Great Barrier Reef / learn to dive)
2. I'd like to ______________________ .
   (get tickets to the Sydney Opera House / see a concert)
3. We're going ______________________ .
   (fly to the outback / go walking)
4. I'd like ______________________ .
   (visit Tasmania / see some friends)
5. I need ______________________ .
   (go online / find some cheap hotels)
6. We want ______________________ .
   (go shopping / buy some opal jewelry)

## 3 Online forum

Grammar | **Complete the questions on the online forum. Then answer the questions with true information about your town or city.**

**Visitor's Center Forum**

1. **From:** clueless *Is it important to bring a guidebook?* (important / bring a guidebook)
   **From:** travelsmart *Yes, it is, and it's also useful to bring a phrase book.*
2. **From:** nocreditcard ______________________ (safe / carry cash)
   **From:** travelsmart ______________________
3. **From:** walksalot ______________________ (expensive / rent a car)
   **From:** travelsmart ______________________
4. **From:** concernedtourist ______________________ (easy / find cheap restaurants)
   **From:** travelsmart ______________________
5. **From:** wiseowl ______________________ (hard / get around)
   **From:** travelsmart ______________________
6. **From:** advanceplanner ______________________ (necessary / make hotel reservations)
   **From:** travelsmart ______________________

# 1 What is it?

Vocabulary **A Write the words under the pictures.**

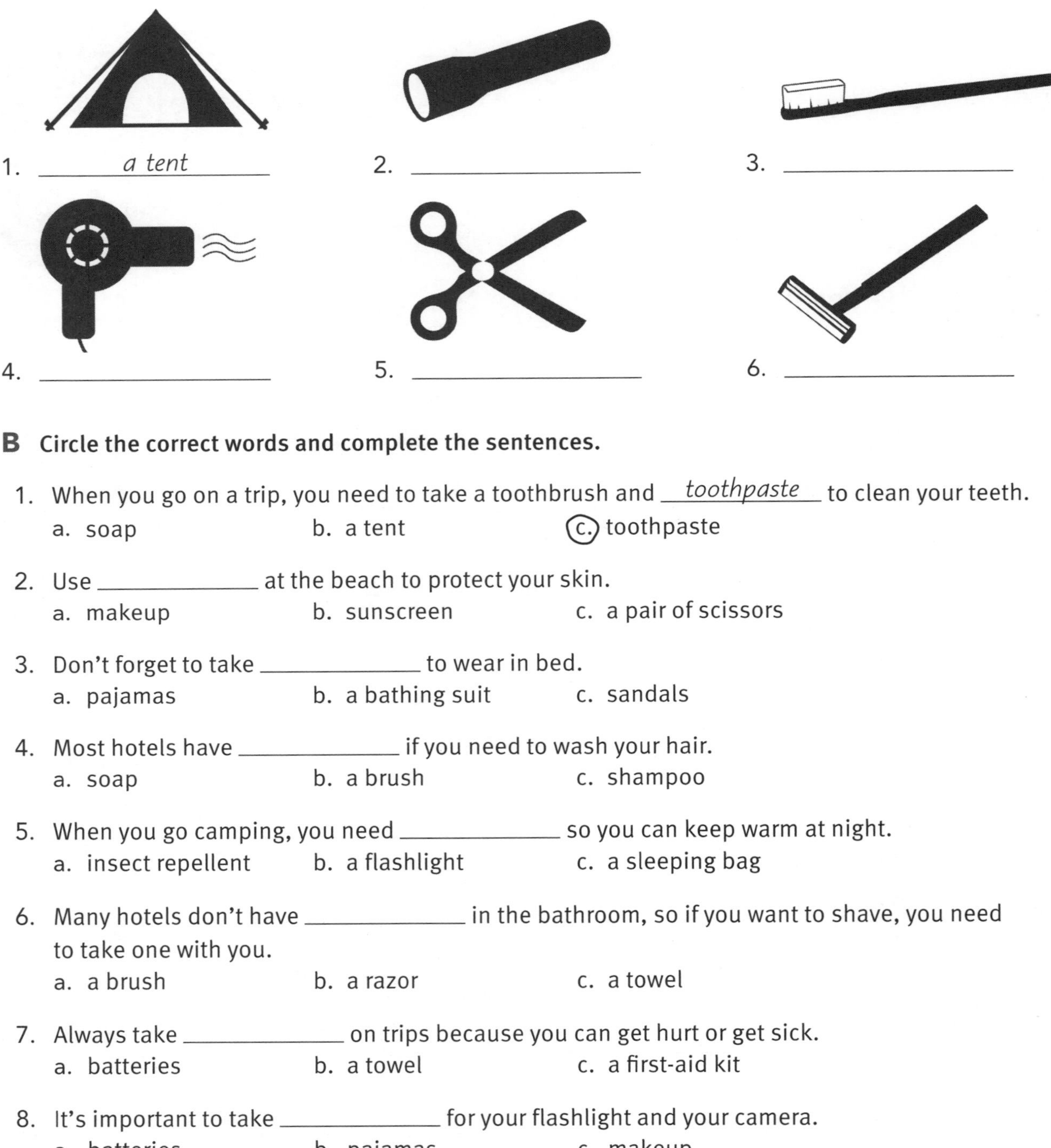

1. *a tent*
2. ____________
3. ____________
4. ____________
5. ____________
6. ____________

**B Circle the correct words and complete the sentences.**

1. When you go on a trip, you need to take a toothbrush and *toothpaste* to clean your teeth.
   a. soap b. a tent (c.) toothpaste
2. Use ____________ at the beach to protect your skin.
   a. makeup b. sunscreen c. a pair of scissors
3. Don't forget to take ____________ to wear in bed.
   a. pajamas b. a bathing suit c. sandals
4. Most hotels have ____________ if you need to wash your hair.
   a. soap b. a brush c. shampoo
5. When you go camping, you need ____________ so you can keep warm at night.
   a. insect repellent b. a flashlight c. a sleeping bag
6. Many hotels don't have ____________ in the bathroom, so if you want to shave, you need to take one with you.
   a. a brush b. a razor c. a towel
7. Always take ____________ on trips because you can get hurt or get sick.
   a. batteries b. a towel c. a first-aid kit
8. It's important to take ____________ for your flashlight and your camera.
   a. batteries b. pajamas c. makeup
9. Wear ____________ to keep your feet cool when it's hot.
   a. sunglasses b. sandals c. a hat
10. Always wear ____________ if there are insects and mosquitoes.
    a. sunscreen b. makeup c. insect repellent

## 2 I think you should . . .

Grammar **Circle the correct words to complete the advice. Then add your own advice in the spaces below.**

1. A We're going hiking in the mountains this weekend. What should we take?
   B Well, you should **to take** / **take** insect repellent and a first-aid kit.
   *You want to wear good hiking boots, too.*
2. A We're going skiing for the first time next month.
   B You know, it's easy to get a sunburn. **Don't forget** / **Why don't you** to use sunscreen.
   ______________________________
3. A I want to go backpacking in Asia on my next vacation.
   B Then you need **pack** / **to pack** a lot of light clothes.
   ______________________________
4. A My mother and I are planning a shopping trip in Hong Kong.
   B Then you really **could** / **should** take an empty suitcase with you.
   ______________________________
5. A It's my friend's birthday on Friday. She's planning an all-night party.
   B In that case, **to take** / **take** your pajamas with you.
   ______________________________
6. A I'm going on a camping trip, but I'm scared of the dark.
   B **Do you want** / **Why don't you** take a flashlight?
   ______________________________
7. A I'm really excited about my trip to Paris. We're going to do a lot of walking.
   B You shouldn't **to forget** / **forget** to take some comfortable shoes then.
   ______________________________
8. A I'm starting a dance class next week, but I don't have the right shoes.
   B You could **borrow** / **to borrow** your sister's shoes.
   ______________________________

## 3 Travel suggestions

Grammar and vocabulary **Give some advice to a tourist on vacation in your country. Complete the sentences with your own ideas.**

1. Don't forget *to pack a bathing suit* .
2. It's a good idea ______________ .
3. You could ______________ .
4. You shouldn't ______________ .
5. Why don't you ______________ .
6. You should ______________ .

# That's a great idea.

## 1 Responding to suggestions

Conversation strategies

**Who really likes each suggestion? Circle *a* or *b*.**

1. Let's go out for sushi tomorrow.
   (a.) That's a great idea.
   b. I don't know. I don't really like fish.

2. We should go hiking together sometime.
   a. I'd love to! When?
   b. Maybe someday.

3. Why don't we get some tickets and see a show?
   a. I don't know. Theater tickets are pretty expensive.
   b. That sounds like fun. What do you want to see?

4. Would you like to go shopping for souvenirs this morning?
   a. That sounds like a good idea. Where do you want to go?
   b. Yeah, maybe we should do that sometime.

5. Let's drive through South America next summer.
   a. I'd like to, but I need to get a part-time job.
   b. That's an interesting idea. Let's do it.

## 2 That sounds great.

Conversation strategies

**Write two responses to each suggestion. Write a response to show you like the suggestion. Then write a response to show you don't like it.**

1. A Let's drive up to the mountains next weekend.
   B *That sounds great. When should we leave?*
   *I don't know. It's pretty cold this time of year.*

2. A We could take a semester off from school and go backpacking.
   B ______________________________
   ______________________________

3. A Why don't we go snorkeling sometime?
   B ______________________________
   ______________________________

4. A We should go camping next spring.
   B ______________________________
   ______________________________

5. A Why don't we just stay home, watch TV, and relax over the winter break?
   B ______________________________
   ______________________________

## 3 I guess . . .

Conversation strategies

**Circle the correct use of *I guess*. There is only one in each sentence. Cross out the others.**

1. Maria Would you like to go dancing tomorrow night?
   Nick I have to ~~I guess~~ work, but (I guess) I could go on Sunday night.
2. Lucy Why don't you come to the beach with me this weekend?
   Emi **I guess** I should get **I guess** away. But I should **I guess** study for my exams, **I guess**.
3. Tania Let's eat out tonight. I'd like to try that new Mexican restaurant downtown.
   Sylvia We could **I guess** try it, **I guess**, but I really **I guess** feel like Italian tonight.
4. Olivia I went to India last summer, and the food was amazing! I loved it!
   Chad Yeah, it's good. **I guess** I could **I guess** make some Indian food tonight.
5. Marc Mandy and I have four tickets to a Broadway show on Friday. You and Mari should come with us.
   Taka We could, **I guess**, but we don't **I guess** have a babysitter.

## 4 Let's see a movie.

Conversation strategies

**Unscramble the suggestions. Write your own responses using *I guess*. Add more information.**

1. tonight / Let's / after class / see a movie .
   *Let's see a movie after class tonight.*
   *I guess we could. I don't have any plans.*
2. drive / Why / to the beach / don't we ?
   ____________________
   ____________________
3. grandmother / visit / this weekend / Let's / my .
   ____________________
   ____________________
4. don't we / in the mountains / go camping / Why ?
   ____________________
   ____________________
5. could / We / a couple of weeks / for / to Europe / go .
   ____________________
   ____________________
6. want to / meet / Do / my / you / parents ?
   ____________________
   ____________________

# Lesson D Interesting places

## 1 A trip of a lifetime

Reading **A Read the article. Write the correct heading for each paragraph.**

**A** Salt, Salt Everywhere **B** A Place to Chill Out **C** Dive into the Lobby

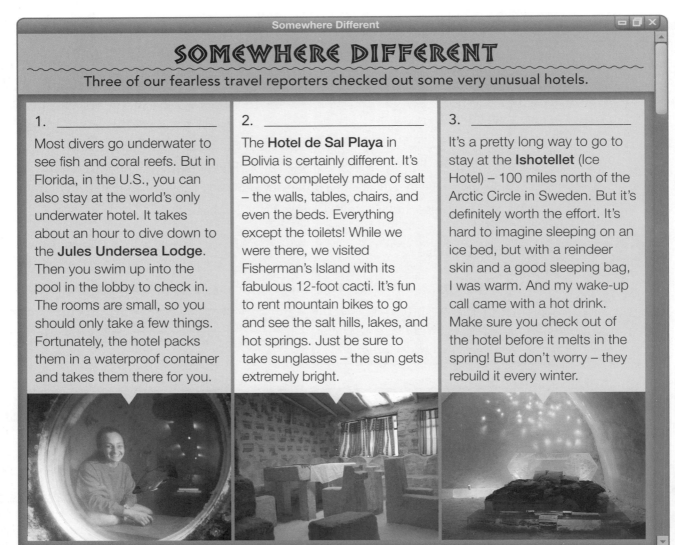

Somewhere Different

### SOMEWHERE DIFFERENT

Three of our fearless travel reporters checked out some very unusual hotels.

1. ______________

Most divers go underwater to see fish and coral reefs. But in Florida, in the U.S., you can also stay at the world's only underwater hotel. It takes about an hour to dive down to the **Jules Undersea Lodge**. Then you swim up into the pool in the lobby to check in. The rooms are small, so you should only take a few things. Fortunately, the hotel packs them in a waterproof container and takes them there for you.

2. ______________

The **Hotel de Sal Playa** in Bolivia is certainly different. It's almost completely made of salt – the walls, tables, chairs, and even the beds. Everything except the toilets! While we were there, we visited Fisherman's Island with its fabulous 12-foot cacti. It's fun to rent mountain bikes to go and see the salt hills, lakes, and hot springs. Just be sure to take sunglasses – the sun gets extremely bright.

3. ______________

It's a pretty long way to go to stay at the **Ishotellet** (Ice Hotel) – 100 miles north of the Arctic Circle in Sweden. But it's definitely worth the effort. It's hard to imagine sleeping on an ice bed, but with a reindeer skin and a good sleeping bag, I was warm. And my wake-up call came with a hot drink. Make sure you check out of the hotel before it melts in the spring! But don't worry – they rebuild it every winter.

**B Read the article again. Find the information.**

1. How do you get to the Jules Undersea Lodge? *You dive underwater to get to it.*
2. How long does it take to get to the Jules Undersea Lodge? ______________
3. What are three interesting things to see near the Hotel de Sal Playa? ______________
4. Why do you need sunglasses at the Hotel de Sal Playa? ______________
5. Where do you sleep at the Ice Hotel? ______________
6. Why do they have to rebuild the Ice Hotel every year? ______________

## 2 An email from Ireland

Writing | **A Read Annie's email to Beth. Then match the email sections to the correct sentences.**

- Say something you are going to do.
- Describe the place, food, or weather.
- End the email.
- Start the email.
- Say something you did.
- Say if you're enjoying your stay.
- Attach a photo and describe it.

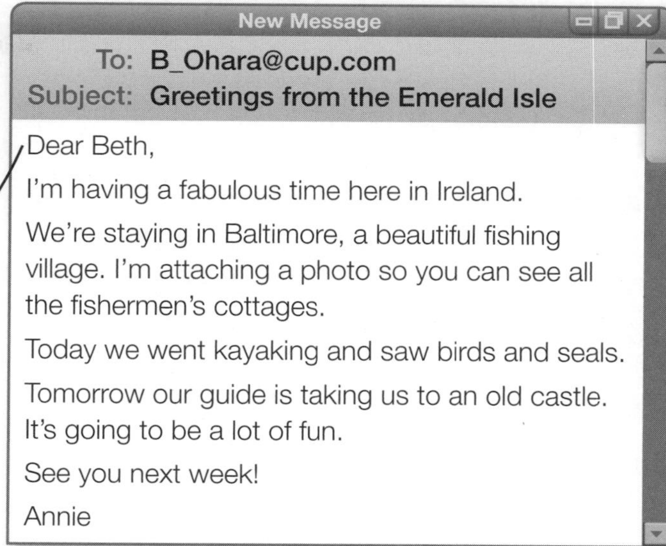

New Message

To: B_Ohara@cup.com

Subject: Greetings from the Emerald Isle

Dear Beth,

I'm having a fabulous time here in Ireland.

We're staying in Baltimore, a beautiful fishing village. I'm attaching a photo so you can see all the fishermen's cottages.

Today we went kayaking and saw birds and seals.

Tomorrow our guide is taking us to an old castle. It's going to be a lot of fun.

See you next week!

Annie

**B Write an email to a friend. Tell him or her about a place you visited once.**

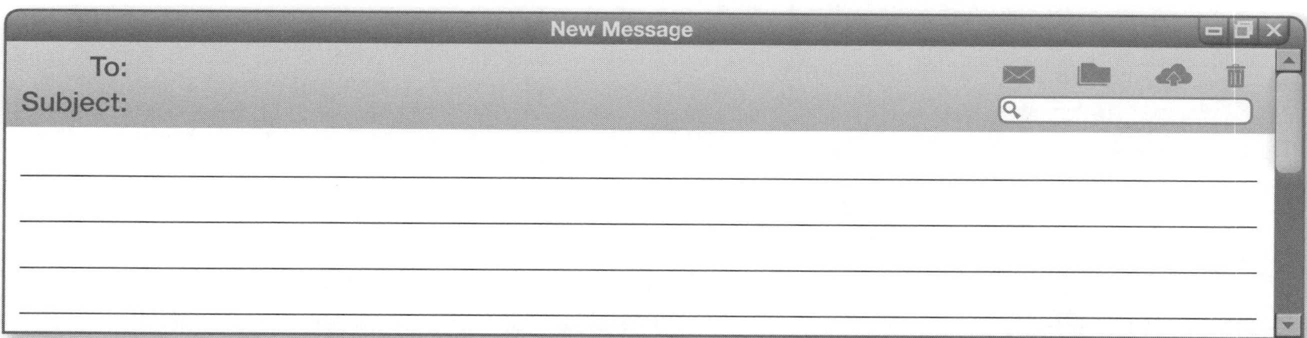


## Unit 7 Progress chart

| | What can you do? Mark the boxes. ✓ = I can . . . ? = I need to review how to . . . | To review, go back to these pages in the Student's Book. |
|---|---|---|
| Grammar | ☐ use infinitives to give reasons. | 66 and 67 |
| | ☐ use *It's* + adjective + *to* . . . | 66 and 67 |
| | ☐ ask for and give advice and suggestions. | 69 |
| Vocabulary | ☐ name at least 5 things to do to get ready for a trip. | 66 and 67 |
| | ☐ name at least 12 things to pack for different kinds of trips. | 68 and 69 |
| Conversation strategies | ☐ respond to suggestions I like and don't like. | 70 and 71 |
| | ☐ use *I guess* when I'm unsure about something. | 71 |
| Writing | ☐ format and use correct expressions in an email. | 73 |

# At home

UNIT 8

## Lesson A Spring cleaning

### Whose is it?

Grammar and vocabulary

**A Complete the chart with the correct pronouns.**

| Subject pronouns | Object pronouns | Possessive adjectives | Possessive pronouns |
|---|---|---|---|
| I | *me* | | *mine* |
| you | | | |
| he | | *his* | |
| she | | | |
| we | | | |
| they | | | |

**B Look at the pictures and write questions with *Whose*. Then answer the questions using possessive pronouns.**

1. A *Whose suitcases are those?*
   B *They're ours.*

2. A ________________
   B ________________

3. A ________________
   B ________________

4. A ________________
   B ________________

5. A ________________
   B ________________

6. A ________________
   B ________________

## 2 After the party

Grammar | **Circle the correct words to complete the conversation.**

Karen Wow! What a mess.
Matt Are all of these things **our** / **ours** (circled)?
Karen No, they're things people forgot when they left the party last night.
Matt Well, I'm looking for **my** / **mine** jacket.
Karen Is this **your** / **yours** jacket?
Matt No, that's not **my** / **mine**. **My** / **Mine** is blue. I guess that's Felipe's.
Karen No, it's not **him** / **his**. Felipe's jacket's gray.
Matt Oh, well. Wow! Look at those DVDs. Whose are they?
Karen I think they're your parents'. Yeah, these are **their** / **theirs**. We borrowed them when we were at **their** / **theirs** house last weekend.
Matt Oh, yeah, . . . right. Hey, whose keys are these? Are they Jan's?
Karen No, they're not **her** / **hers**. See the keychain? It says "Andy."
Matt I lost **my** / **mine** glasses, too!
Karen Wait a minute. Is this jacket **your** / **yours**?
Matt Yes, thanks! You're amazing. Now, do you think you can find **my** / **mine** glasses?

## 3 About you

Grammar and vocabulary | **Are these sentences true or false for you? Write *T* (true) or *F* (false). Then correct the false sentences.**

1. I can never find anything in my closet. _F_
   *I can usually find things in my closet, but I can't find things in my drawers.*
2. All my pens are in a jar on my desk. _____
   ______________________________
3. I put things like my ID card and passport in a drawer in my dresser. _____
   ______________________________
4. There's a box under my bed with photos and letters in it. _____
   ______________________________
5. I put all my old magazines and books in the closet. _____
   ______________________________
6. I keep stuff like shampoo, brushes, and my hair dryer in a drawer. _____
   ______________________________
7. I keep all my shoes in the closet. _____
   ______________________________

# Lesson B Things at home

## 1 Rooms and things

Vocabulary **A** There are 20 home items in the puzzle. Find the other 18. Look in these directions (→↓).

| Q | A | R | M | C | H | A | I | R | Q | W | T | B | A |
|---|---|---|---|---|---|---|---|---|---|---|---|---|---|
| R | U | B | H | T | K | V | P | G | H | M | L | A | J |
| L | E | C | A | R | P | E | T | U | K | I | Y | T | K |
| E | K | F | S | S | A | L | Q | W | E | R | R | H | C |
| S | D | I | S | H | W | A | S | H | E | R | F | T | C |
| E | R | S | T | O | V | M | O | A | P | O | B | U | U |
| R | E | C | O | W | T | P | F | E | M | R | G | B | R |
| C | S | O | V | E | N | N | A | F | A | U | C | E | T |
| A | S | A | E | R | B | U | K | R | W | C | L | O | A |
| B | E | M | I | C | R | O | W | A | V | E | Z | A | I |
| I | R | Q | U | X | L | S | I | N | K | I | K | Z | N |
| N | M | N | I | G | H | T | S | T | A | N | D | E | S |
| E | S | E | C | U | S | H | I | O | N | S | R | X | Z |
| T | O | I | L | E | T | R | E | S | Y | L | V | A | D |
| S | F | A | C | O | F | F | E | E | T | A | B | L | E |

**B** Read the clues and write the rooms in the center of the webs. Then complete the webs with words from part A. Some words can be used more than once.

1. I sleep in this room.

2. I cook and sometimes eat in this room.

3. I wash my face and brush my teeth in this room.

4. In this room, I listen to music, watch TV, and relax.

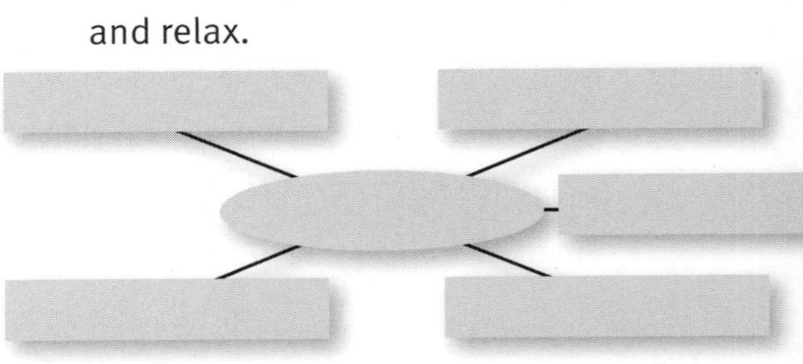

## 2 I like that one.

Grammar | **Look at the pictures. Complete Ana's questions with *one* or *ones*. Bob has different tastes. Write his answers using two adjectives and a prepositional phrase.**

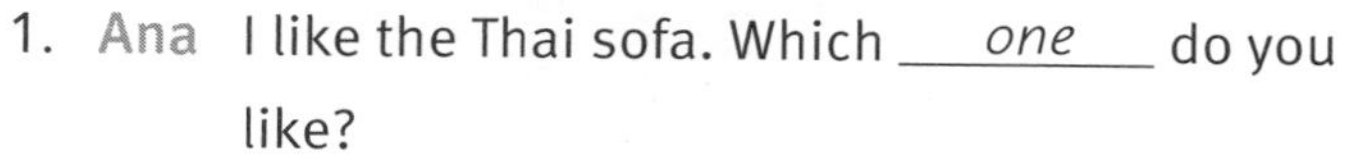

1. Ana I like the Thai sofa. Which ___one___ do you like?
   Bob ___Oh, I like the big Italian one on the right.___

2. Ana I like the white dresser. Which ________ do you like?
   Bob ________________________________

3. Ana I like the square mirrors. Which ________ do you like?
   Bob ________________________________

4. Ana I love the big clock. Which ________ do you like?
   Bob ________________________________

## 3 Susan's living room

Grammar and vocabulary | **Unscramble the sentences about Susan's living room.**

1. small / living room / There's / a / sofa / in / her
   ___There's a small sofa in her living room.___
2. has / square / some / cool / cushions / She / on the sofa
   ________________________________
3. in front of / There's / a / the / coffee table / sofa / long / dark
   ________________________________
4. a / TV / She / big / on the wall / has / black
   ________________________________
5. lamp / a / There's / tall / in the corner / Italian
   ________________________________
6. are / on the floor / some / cotton / nice / rugs / There
   ________________________________

## 1 Asking politely

Conversation strategies | **Complete the questions with *Would you mind* or *Do you mind if*.**

1. A *Do you mind if* I borrow your dictionary?
   B No, not at all. Go ahead.
2. A ________________ answering the phone for me?
   B Oh, no. No problem.
3. A ________________ closing that door?
   B No, not at all.
4. A ________________ I take off my shoes?
   B No. Go right ahead.
5. A ________________ I use your laptop for a minute?
   B No problem.

6. A ________________ handing me the potato salad?
   B Oh, no. Not at all. Here you go.
7. A ________________ playing that song again?
   B I'd be happy to.
8. A ________________ I eat the last piece of apple pie?
   B Not at all. Go ahead.
9. A ________________ I turn on the news for a minute?
   B No, not at all.
10. A ________________ turning down the music a little?
    B No problem.

## 2 No problem.

Conversation strategies **Circle the correct responses to complete the conversation.**

Mother Rudy, do you have a minute?

Rudy **Sure.** / **No, not at all.** What's the matter?

Mother Well, your grandparents are on their way, and the house is a mess. Could you please clean your room before they get here?

Rudy **No, go right ahead.** / **OK.** I can do it now.

Mother Oh, and would you mind taking your weight-training things out of the living room?

Rudy **Sure. No problem.** / **Yes.** But do you mind if I do it after I clean my room?

Mother **No, of course not.** / **Sure, I'd be happy to.** Actually, I should probably call your grandparents to make sure they're not lost. Where's my phone?

Rudy Um, I don't know.

Mother Hmm. Can I borrow your phone for a minute?

Rudy **No. Go right ahead.** / **Sure, go ahead.**

Mother Where is it?

Rudy Uh . . . I don't know. I think it's here somewhere. . . .

## 3 Requests, requests

Conversation strategies **Agree to these requests from a visitor to your home. Then add a question.**

1. A I feel sleepy. Would you mind making some coffee?
   B *No, not at all. How you do like it?*
2. A Do you mind if we watch the soccer game tonight?
   B ______
3. A I feel hot. Could I get a glass of water?
   B ______
4. A Can I borrow your phone? I need to call my sister.
   B ______
5. A Sorry, I can't hear you. Would you mind turning down the music a little?
   B ______
6. A Can we listen to some music?
   B ______
7. A I feel a little hungry. Do you mind if I take an apple?
   B ______
8. A Could I borrow a sweater? I feel a little cold.
   B ______

# Lesson D Home habits

## Cat habitat

Reading **A What do you think these words mean?**

cat boat | cat lady | houseboat | stray cat

**B Read the article and check the meanings of the words in part A.**

### *All aboard, furry neighbors!*

Have you ever lived next door to a boat? How about a boat full of cats?

Amsterdam, the largest city in the Netherlands, is full of canals. There are many different kinds of boats on the canals. Some of them carry people and goods, some have shops or restaurants on them, while others are houseboats – boats that people live on. But not only people live on these houseboats. Cats do too, at least on two of them.

It all began in 1966 with a stray cat, her kittens, and a kind woman named Henriette van Weelde. One rainy night, Henriette heard a cat crying outside her house. She opened the door and saw a wet mother cat trying to protect her kittens from the rain. Henriette felt sorry for the poor animals, so she let them live with her. Soon another stray cat joined them, and then more. Henriette quickly became known as the "cat lady."

Before long, the cats filled Henriette's house. Then they filled her garden. And the cats kept coming. What could she do with them all? She saw the answer to her problem floating on the canal – a houseboat. People could live on houseboats, so why couldn't cats? In 1968, Henriette bought her first "cat boat."

Soon, even more stray cats moved in, and then came people who wanted to help – the first volunteers. But after just three years, the houseboat was full of cats. So Henriette bought another boat! More people were visiting, not just to bring cats in, but also to adopt a pet or just to look. After all, a houseboat for cats is not a common sight!

Today, Henriette's two cat boats are still in the same place on the canal. And the Cat Boat Foundation that Henriette started years ago is not only an official Dutch charity but also an international tourist attraction!

**C Read these questions. Find the answers in the article.**

1. What do the boats on Amsterdam's canals do? *They carry people and goods. Some of them are shops and restaurants. People live on them, too.*
2. Why did Henriette van Weelde take in the first stray cat? ______
3. What did Henriette do when her house and garden filled with cats? ______
4. Who helped Henriette take care of the cats? ______
5. What are two reasons people visit Henriette's cat boats? ______

## 2 A typical Sunday

Writing **A Read the statements. Choose the correct words to complete the sentences.**

1. *First*, Danny wakes up around noon on Sunday. (first / as soon as)
2. He sleeps for 30 or so minutes more ________ he gets out of bed. (before / after)
3. ________, he takes a quick shower, gets dressed, and goes downstairs. (then / while)
4. ________, he goes into the kitchen and makes a huge breakfast. (when / next)
5. ________ he's eating breakfast, he reads the sports section of the paper. (during / while)
6. He checks his email ________ he finishes his breakfast. (when / next)
7. He watches football on TV ________ he's off the computer. (as soon as / then)
8. He usually falls asleep once or twice ________ the game. (during / while)
9. ________ the game is over, Danny goes upstairs and takes a long nap. (then / after)

**B Write true sentences about your Sunday afternoons. Use *first, next, then, before, after, during, as soon as, while,* and *when*.**

*First, I*

## Unit 8 Progress chart

| | What can you do? Mark the boxes. ✓ = I can . . . ? = I need to review how to . . . | To review, go back to these pages in the Student's Book. |
|---|---|---|
| Grammar | ☐ ask questions with *Whose*. | 76 and 77 |
| | ☐ use possessive pronouns. | 76 and 77 |
| | ☐ order adjectives before nouns, and before the pronouns *one* and *ones*. | 79 |
| | ☐ use location expressions after nouns and pronouns. | 79 |
| Vocabulary | ☐ name at least 6 places to keep things in my home. | 75 |
| | ☐ name at least 15 home items for different rooms. | 78 |
| Conversation strategies | ☐ request permission politely to do things with *Do you mind if . . . ?* | 80 and 81 |
| | ☐ make requests politely with *Would you mind . . . ?* | 80 and 81 |
| | ☐ agree to requests in different ways. | 81 |
| Writing | ☐ order events using sequencing words. | 83 |

# Things happen

UNIT 9

## Lesson A When things go wrong . . .

### 1 What were they doing?

Grammar **Circle the correct verb forms in these stories.**

1. A friend and I **ran** / **were running** in the park, and this guy **rode** / **was riding** behind us. We didn't hear him because we **listened** / **were listening** to music. Anyway, we **decided** / **were deciding** to stop because I was tired, and the guy **ran** / **was running** right into me. And then he just **rode** / **was riding** away!

2. An embarrassing thing **happened** / **was happening** when I **studied** / **was studying** singing at the university. At my first concert, I was on the stage and I **saw** / **was seeing** a concert hall full of people. I **got** / **was getting** so scared that I completely **forgot** / **was forgetting** the words to my song. So I just **stood** / **was standing** on the stage, and I **said** / **was saying**, "Thank you." After that, I **walked** / **was walking** off and **went** / **was going** home.

### 2 Interruptions

Grammar **Complete the stories with the verbs given. Use one simple past verb and one past continuous verb in each sentence.**

1. I *was telling* (tell) my friends a funny story about my brother, and he ____________ (walk) in.
2. I ____________ (do) my laundry, and I ____________ (hear) a noise. My phone was in the washing machine.
3. My dad ____________ (delete) my music files when he ____________ (try) to fix my computer.
4. A friend and I ____________ (have) lunch when our server ____________ (spill) coffee all over us.
5. My mom and dad ____________ (saw) one of their neighbors on the same plane when they ____________ (fly) to Beijing.
6. My teacher ____________ (talk) on her cell phone, and she ____________ (run) right into me in the hallway.

# 3 Telling anecdotes

Grammar and vocabulary **Look at the pictures. Write sentences using the past continuous and the simple past.**

1. *A guy was having his lunch in the park. He was reading.* ________________________________________________________________________________________________________________________________________________________________________________________

2. ____________________________________________________________________________________________________________________________________________________________________________

# 4 About you

Grammar **Think about your week. Complete the sentences with true information.**

1. When I was eating dinner a couple of nights ago, *I spilled spaghetti sauce on my favorite T-shirt* .
2. My friend called me when I ____________________________ last weekend.
3. I was doing my homework one night when ____________________________ .
4. Last week, I was going to class, and I ____________________________ .
5. Last weekend, I ____________________________ when I ____________________________ .
6. Yesterday, I was talking to a friend and ____________________________ .

# 1 Parts of the body

Reading **A** Look at the pictures and complete the puzzle.

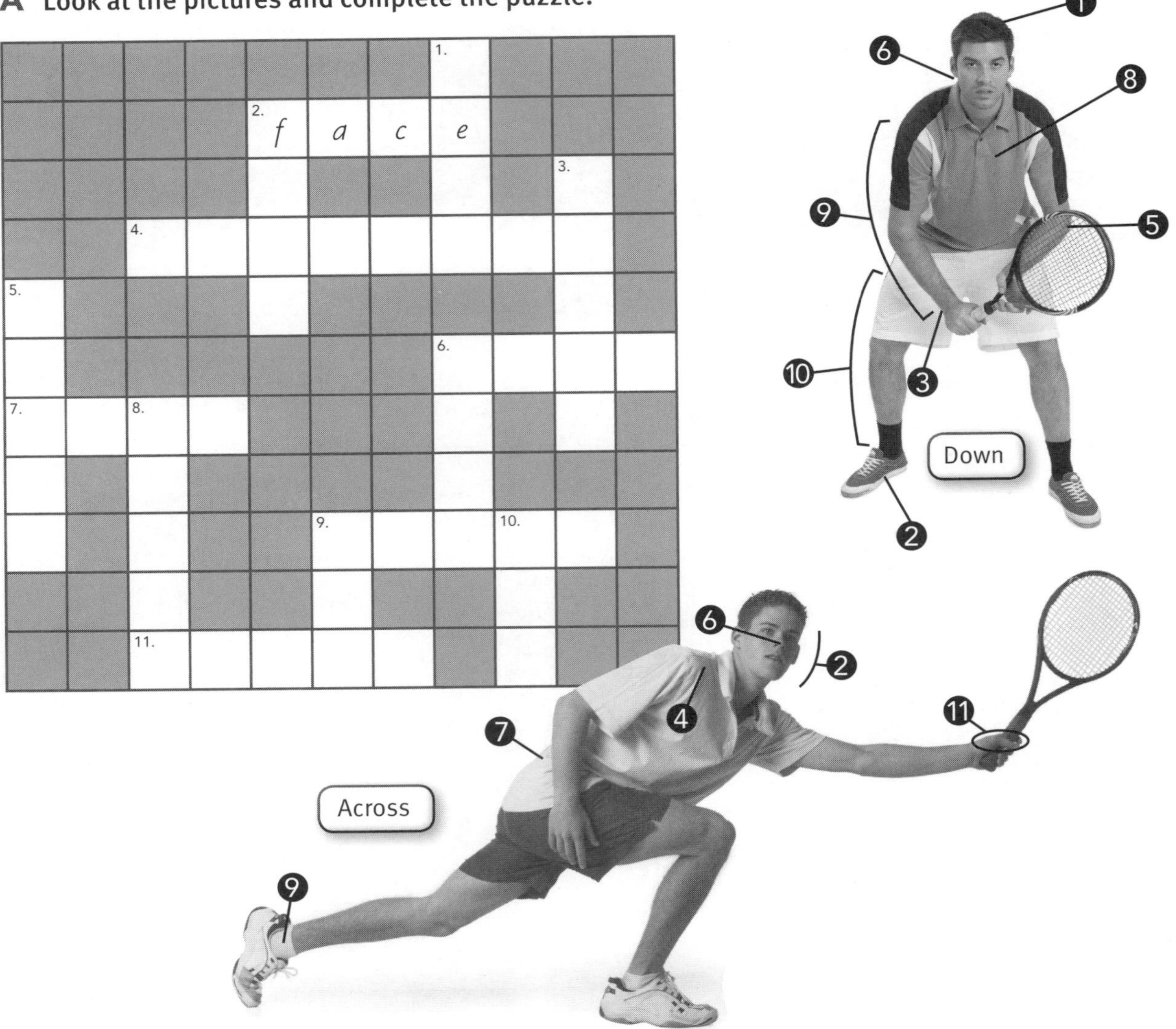


**B** Circle the correct words and complete the sentences.

1. I can't move. I hurt my *back* .
   a. thumb (b.) back c. arm
2. It's hard to walk. I broke my ________ .
   a. nose b. leg c. shoulder
3. I got a bruise on my ________ . It hurts to smile.
   a. finger b. toe c. face
4. I sprained my ________ , so it's hard to write.
   a. wrist b. ankle c. chest
5. It hurts to wear high heels. I broke my ________ .
   a. finger b. shoulder c. toe
6. I got a black ________ . I can't see clearly.
   a. eye b. head c. neck
7. I can't bend my arm. I hurt my ________ .
   a. elbow b. hip c. knee
8. It's hard to wash dishes. I cut my ________ .
   a. knee b. foot c. hand
9. I hurt my ________ . I can't turn my head.
   a. thumb b. neck c. wrist
10. I broke my ________ . It's hard to breathe.
    a. nose b. hip c. eye

## 2 How did you hurt yourself?

Grammar | **Complete the conversations. Use reflexive pronouns.**

1. A How did your sister hurt her hand?
   B Oh, she burned __________ when she was making tea.

2. A Are you OK? Did you hurt your ankle?
   B Yeah. I fell when I was jogging. I didn't hurt __________ badly.

3. A What happened to your friends?
   B Oh, they hurt __________ when they were moving to a new apartment.

4. A How did your father cut __________?
   B He was chopping vegetables for dinner.

## 3 A wonderful day

Grammar | **Complete the conversation. Write the questions using the past continuous.**

Mom Hi, honey. How was your day?

Alicia Well, I hurt myself. I kicked a ball, and it hit me on the head.

Mom Oh, no! *What were you doing?* (What)

Alicia Well, I was playing soccer with some friends. I was looking in the other direction.

Mom ______________________ (Why)

Alicia Well, I was looking at a guy. I guess I wasn't paying attention.

Mom ______________________ (Who)

Alicia This really cute guy named Jason.

Mom ______________________ (Was)

Alicia No, he wasn't playing with us. He was just standing there.

Mom ______________________ (Where)

Alicia In front of the field. He was talking on the phone. Anyway, I kicked the ball, the ball hit Jason, and then it hit me.

Mom That's terrible!

Alicia Not really. Now I have a date with him on Saturday!

## 1 I bet you felt bad!

Conversation strategies | **Number the sentences in the conversation in the correct order.**

1. ____ Australia? That sounds like a fun trip.
   __1__ You won't believe what I did last week. I was riding my bike with a friend in City Park.
   ____ Yeah. But anyway, I wasn't paying attention and ran right into a woman in front of me.
   ____ Yeah, it is. Anyway, my friend and I were talking about going to Australia.
   ____ Oh, that's a beautiful park.
   ____ Oh, no! I bet she wasn't too happy!

2. ____ Yeah. So I jumped out of bed, got dressed, and ran all the way to school.
   ____ You're kidding! That late?
   ____ I bet no one even noticed.
   ____ Yeah, I was. And when I got to class, I saw that I was wearing two different sneakers. One blue and one black! But anyway, everyone was studying for a test. So I just sat at the back.
   ____ Guess what I did? I woke up late this morning, and it was after 10:30.
   ____ The whole way? I bet you were exhausted!

3. ____ I know. The horse fell right on top of her, and she couldn't get up. But my father was there.
   ____ Yeah, it was. My dad took her to the hospital, and she's OK now.
   ____ Do you remember my cousin, Courtney? Well, one day last summer she was out riding when her horse fell.
   ____ That was lucky!
   ____ Oh, my gosh! That's awful.
   ____ Thank goodness.

## 2 I bet . . .

Conversation strategies **Complete each conversation with an appropriate response using *I bet*.**

1. A I was at the mall the other day, and I walked right into a glass door! I was so embarrassed.
   B *I bet no one even noticed.*
2. A My sister wasn't paying attention when she left home for work this morning, and she locked herself out of her apartment.
   B ______________________________
3. A My little sister borrowed my new laptop last night, and she dropped it! So now it's not working.
   B ______________________________
4. A I went to a concert with some friends last weekend, but I was so bored that I fell asleep!
   B ______________________________
5. A I went to the car wash yesterday and forgot to close the car window. I got so wet!
   B ______________________________
6. A Guess what? I just won a trip to Miami in a radio contest!
   B ______________________________

## 3 And then what happened?

Conversation strategies **Finish these anecdotes. Then write an appropriate response.**

1. A I was walking to work one morning, and I thought I saw my old friend from middle school across the street. *So I ran after him and called his name. Anyway, he turned around and it wasn't my friend at all.*
   B *Oh, no! I bet you were embarrassed.*
2. A I was taking a taxi once, and I was in a hurry. I wanted to pay with my credit card but ______________________________
   ______________________________
   ______________________________
   B ______________________________
3. A Last year, none of my friends called to wish me Happy Birthday. I thought, "Maybe they just forgot." Well, when I got home, I opened the door and ______________________________
   ______________________________
   B ______________________________
4. A My brother was driving my dad's car in a bad storm one night and ______________________________
   ______________________________
   ______________________________
   B ______________________________

# Lesson D Happy endings

## Acts of kindness

Reading **A Read the article. Find the answers to these questions.**

1. Who is Nelson Hunter?
2. Who found Andrea's wallet?
3. How did Abby get home?
4. What did John get?

### Around Town *by Nelson Hunter*

A few weeks ago, I was walking to my car in the parking lot, when someone came up to me and said he enjoyed reading my weekly column. "But," he said, "you always write about everyone's bad experiences. Why don't you ask people to talk about their good experiences, too?"

So I asked readers to write in and tell me about all the good things that happened to them recently. I got hundreds of replies. Here are three of them:

When I was shopping at the mall last week, I lost my wallet with all my money and credit cards in it. I spent a long time looking for it with no luck. I was really upset because it had my spare house key and my address in it, too. Anyway, later that day after I got home, my doorbell rang. It was a young man, and he had my wallet. Apparently, he saw it on the ground when he was walking into the mall. He drove all the way to my house to give it to me! I couldn't believe it! I was so lucky!

– Andrea Keane

I was coming home from a party really late at night, and I missed the last train home. I didn't have enough money for a cab, and I didn't want to walk home in the dark. I was standing outside the train station, and I guess I looked worried because a woman came up and asked me if I needed any help. She offered to share a cab with me and to pay for it! She said she didn't like being by herself at night, either. I was so grateful.

– Abby Walters

After class each week, I often go to the local donut shop and get some coffee before I go home. When I was leaving the store last week, the owner gave me a bag of donuts from the day before to take home for free. She said I was a good customer, and she didn't want to throw them out. When I got home, I shared them with my roommates!

– John Jones

So, thank you for all the letters. For next week, I want to hear about any funny stories you have. What funny things happened to you recently?

**B Read the article again. Write *T* (true) or *F* (false) for each sentence. Then correct the false sentences.**

1. Nelson Hunter usually writes about bad things that happen to people. T
2. Andrea was worried because if someone found her wallet, they could get into her house. ____
3. A young man found Andrea's wallet when he was leaving the mall. ____
4. Abby Walters had to pay for a cab home when she missed her train. ____
5. John ate the bag of donuts by himself. ____

## 2 Two unusual events

Writing **A Read about two unusual events. Complete the stories using *when* or *while*. Sometimes both are correct.**

❶ Years ago, *when* my friend and I were in middle school, we decided to write our names on a one-dollar bill for fun. We spent the money and forgot about it. Then, one night about 20 years later, ________ I was waiting for a bus, I saw a dollar bill on the street. I picked it up, and my name was on it. It was the same bill we wrote on! ________ I think of it now, I'm amazed!

– Ken Leonard, Los Angeles

❷ I had a strange experience a couple of months ago. It happened one night ________ I was sleeping. It was probably about two in the morning ________ I woke up to loud music. ________ I looked around, I saw that the radio was on. I clearly remember turning it off ________ I went to bed.

– Lisa Lee, Hong Kong

**B Write about an unusual event that happened to you or to someone you know.**

*A really unusual thing happened to*

## Unit 9 Progress chart

| | What can you do? Mark the boxes.<br>✓ = I can . . . ? = I need to review how to . . . | To review, go back to these pages in the Student's Book. |
|---|---|---|
| Grammar | ☐ make past continuous statements.<br>☐ ask past continuous questions.<br>☐ use reflexive pronouns. | 86 and 87<br>89<br>89 |
| Vocabulary | ☐ name at least 12 parts of the body.<br>☐ name at least 6 injuries. | 88<br>88 and 89 |
| Conversation strategies | ☐ react to and comment on a story.<br>☐ respond with *I bet*. | 90 and 91<br>91 |
| Writing | ☐ link ideas with *when* and *while*. | 93 |

# Lesson A Keeping in touch

## 1 Bigger and better

Grammar **A Complete the chart below with the comparative form of the adjectives in the box.**

| | | | | | |
|---|---|---|---|---|---|
| ✓bad | cheap | easy | hard | noisy | quick |
| big | convenient | expensive | important | old | slow |
| boring | cool | fun | interesting | personal | small |
| busy | difficult | good | new | popular | useful |

| Adjective + *-er* / *-ier* | | *more* / *less* + adjective | | Irregular adjectives | |
|---|---|---|---|---|---|
| | | | | *worse* | |
| | | | | | |
| | | | | | |
| | | | | | |
| | | | | | |
| | | | | | |

**B Complete the sentences with the comparative form of the adjectives.**

1. Postcards are *slower* (slow) than email.
2. Cell-phone service is __________ (expensive) than regular phone service.
3. Texting is often __________ (easy) than sending an email.
4. I think sending e-cards is __________ (convenient) than sending regular cards.
5. To me, black and white photos are __________ (nice) than color photos.
6. I think pop-up ads are __________ (bad) than spam.
7. It's __________ (important) to have a phone than to have a computer.
8. Tablets are __________ (good) than laptops when you're working on the bus.

**C Complete the conversation with the comparative form of the adjectives. Add *than* where necessary. Some adjectives need *less*.**

**Dong-Un** I love my new tablet. It's so much *better than* (good) my old laptop.

**Loni** I know. And the new tablets are __________ (expensive), too. Some cost only $200. Actually, this one was much __________ (cheap) my laptop.

**Dong-Un** And they're __________ (convenient) laptops. They're __________ (fun), too. I like the touch screen. And they have a __________ (long) battery life, too.

**Loni** Right. I know laptops are __________ (popular) tablets these days, but I like my old laptop. It has a __________ (big) memory. And it's __________ (easy) to work on when I have to write long papers.

**Dong-Un** Yeah, but it sure is a lot __________ (heavy) a tablet!

## 2 It's quieter than the office.

Grammar | **Complete the comments with the comparative form of the adjectives. Add *than* where necessary. Some adjectives need *less*.**

1. My boss works on the bus. He says it's *quieter than* (quiet) the office. He thinks there's nothing ____________ (bad) other people's cell phone conversations on the bus.

2. My friend doesn't like e-cards. She says they're ____________ (personal) real cards. Actually, I think they're ____________ (fun) because you can add music and stuff.

3. My dad isn't good with computers. My mom is much ____________ (good) than he is, but she prefers to talk on the phone. She says it's ____________ (easy) to talk and do other things at the same time.

4. My co-workers think video conferencing is ____________ (convenient) business trips. It's also ____________ (tiring) because you don't get jet lag.

## 3 I don't think so!

Grammar and vocabulary | **Write a response to disagree with the statements.**

1. A I think tablets are harder to use than smartphones.
   B *Really? I think tablets are easier to use than smartphones.*
2. A Cameras take better photos than the cameras in cell phones.
   B ________________________________________
3. A I think it's more important to listen to the radio than watch TV.
   B ________________________________________
4. A It's easier to understand a voice-mail message in English than a written note.
   B ________________________________________
5. A It's worse to have no phone than to have no laptop.
   B ________________________________________
6. A I think text messages are more popular than phone calls.
   B ________________________________________

# Lesson B On the phone

## 1 Phone situations

Vocabulary **A Choose the correct word to complete each phone expression.**

| | | a. | b. | c. |
|---|---|---|---|---|
| 1. | call me _c_ | a. number | b. off | c. back |
| 2. | have another ____ | a. call | b. number | c. mistake |
| 3. | leave a ____ | a. back | b. message | c. call |
| 4. | have the wrong ____ | a. number | b. mistake | c. another |
| 5. | hold ____ | a. on | b. in | c. call |
| 6. | get cut ____ | a. back | b. on | c. off |
| 7. | break ____ | a. back | b. up | c. on |

**B Use the phone expressions above to complete the sentences. Use the correct form of the verbs.**

1. One of my friends called me at work, but I was in an important meeting and couldn't talk. I asked him to _call me back_ later.
2. I'm trying to call my sister, but I can't hear her. She's in the mountains, and the call keeps ____________ .
3. I need to talk to my grandmother, but she's not home. I want her to return my call, so I should probably ____________ .
4. My brother tried to call his office, but he accidentally called someone he didn't know. He ____________ .

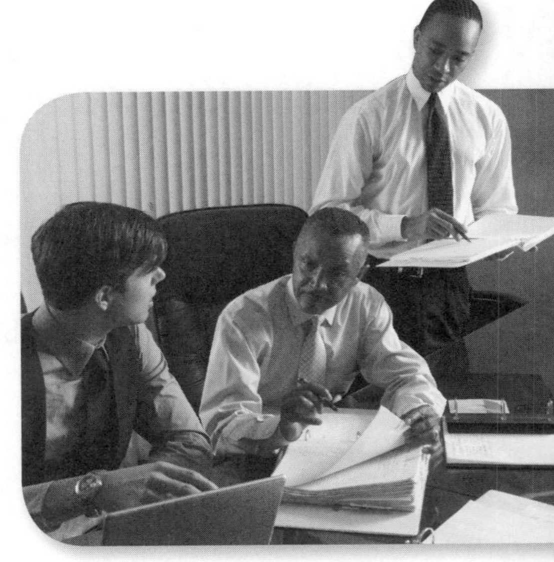

5. I have problems with my cell phone. Every time I walk into my bedroom, I hear a click and then I ____________ .
6. I called my brother, but his wife said he was upstairs watching TV. She asked me to ____________ while she called him to the phone.
7. My mom works at home, and she gets a lot of phone calls. Every time I call her, I have to hold on because she ____________ .

## 2 How do they respond?

Grammar and vocabulary | **Circle the best response for each phone expression.**

1. I can't hear you. You're breaking up.
   a. I have another call.
   b. Call me back later.
2. Please leave a message.
   a. Hi, Frank. This is Manny. Call me at home.
   b. Good-bye.
3. Can you hold on, please?
   a. Sure, no problem.
   b. I got cut off.
4. Oh, I'm sorry. I think I have the wrong number.
   a. One moment, please.
   b. No problem.
5. Good morning, Cambridge University Press.
   a. Would you like to leave a message?
   b. Could I speak to Sally Smith, please?
6. Did you get my message?
   a. Yeah, I think I did.
   b. No problem.

## 3 More than you!

Grammar | **Complete the sentences with *more*, *less*, or *fewer*.**

1. **Nancy** Wow! Look at your inbox. It's full of junk mail. You get a lot ___*more*___ junk mail than I do.
   **Bill** I know. I guess I get a lot of emails, generally. Look – 50 today.
   **Nancy** Yeah. I get about three or four a day. You get a lot ________ emails than I do.
2. **Julie** My cell phone bill was really high this month. I really need to make ________ calls. Or talk ________ than I do now. Look – it was $65.
   **Paula** Actually, that's not bad. Mine was $95. My cell phone costs ________ than yours.
3. **Dan** You know, I only had four text messages last month. I'm getting ________ text messages than phone calls. I guess people prefer to call me these days.
   **Eric** Yeah? Actually, I like instant messaging ________ than talking.
4. **Miki** Are you still working? You spend ________ time online than anyone I know.
   **Larry** I know. I really should work ________ and spend ________ time with you and the kids.
5. **Ben** Oh, no! The Internet is down again! I need to change my Internet service provider to yours. You seem to have ________ problems with your provider than I do.
   **Paul** Maybe. I know my Internet connection goes down ________ than yours, but it costs a lot ________ than yours, too.

## 1 Exciting news

Conversation strategies

**A Read the conversation. Then complete the chart below with expressions from the conversation.**

Ellen: Tommy? It's Ellen. You won't believe it!

Tommy: Sorry, Ellen. Can you hold on a minute? I have to turn the music down. . . . OK, what were you saying?

Ellen: Remember that job interview I had last week?

Tommy: Sure, I do. Oh, just a second. My cell phone's ringing. . . . So, where were we?

Ellen: My job interview last week. They called this morning and – oops! Excuse me just a minute. I spilled my tea. . . . What was I saying?

Tommy: They called about the job. . . .

Ellen: Yeah, right. I got the job! I start next month.

Tommy: Next month? That's great! Oh, just a minute. I need to close the window . . . OK, so you were saying?

Ellen: This is the exciting part! Can you wait just a second? I need to turn off the stove. . . . All right. Where was I?

Tommy: The exciting part about your new job.

Ellen: Right! They want me to work in their London office!

Tommy: That's amazing! Congratulations, Ellen!

| Interrupting a conversation | Restarting a conversation |
|---|---|
| 1. *Can you hold on a minute?* | 1. *OK, what were you saying?* |
| 2. | 2. |
| 3. | 3. |
| 4. | 4. |
| 5. | 5. |

**B Complete the conversations with the expressions from the chart above. Sometimes there is more than one correct answer.**

1. Nolan: Hi, Akemi! I have some good news.
   Akemi: Oh, I'm sorry. ____________ I have another call.
   Nolan: Sure, go ahead.

2. Abby: Kyle, it's Abby. I'm at the supermarket and . . .
   Kyle: Just a second. I have to turn off the TV. ____________
   Abby: I was saying, I'm at the supermarket. Can you come pick me up?

3. Muriel: Hey, it's me. I'm calling because I'm – oops! Hold on, I dropped my briefcase. . . . ____________
   Brett: You're calling because you're . . .
   Muriel: Oh, yes, I'm working late. I'll be home around nine tonight.

## 2 I just need to . . .

Conversation strategies

**Add *just* to the sentences to make them softer.**

1. I need to ask you a few questions. *I just need to ask you a few questions.*
2. Sure. Can you wait a minute? ______
3. I have to answer the door. ______
4. Could you hold on a second? ______
5. I need to turn off the faucet. ______
6. Sorry. I need to take another call. ______
7. I'm calling to find out about your test. ______
8. I have to tell you one thing. ______

## 3 Hold on a second

Conversation strategies

**Imagine a friend calls. Follow the instructions and complete the conversation. Use *just* where possible.**

You: Hello?

Friend: Hi, it's me! Hey, I was just calling to tell you, this weekend there's . . .

You: *Oh, can you hold on a second? I just want to turn down the music.*
*OK. Sorry. So, what were you saying?*
(Interrupt to turn down the music. Restart the conversation.)

Friend: I was just calling to tell you about my party this weekend.

You: Great. So, what's the special . . . ______
______
(Interrupt because you have another call. Ask your friend to call you back.)

Friend: Hey.

You: Hi. Sorry about that. So, ______
(Restart the conversation.)

Friend: My party – this weekend.

You: Right. ______
(Interrupt to answer the door.)

Sorry. So, are you having a birthday party?

Friend: No. It's just for fun. I'm going to invite . . .

You: ______

Oh, that's better.

______
(Interrupt because the call is breaking up. Restart the conversation.)

Friend: Oh, I was saying, I'm going to invite everyone from class. So . . .

You: ______
(Interrupt because your battery is running out. Say you can call back.)

Friend: Hi, again.

You: ______
(Restart the conversation.)

Friend: I was saying that everybody in the class is invited. So, can you come?

You: Oh, yeah, I'd love to. Thanks.

## 1 Drawing crowds

Reading **A Read the definitions of *crowd* and *outsourcing*, and guess the meaning of *crowdsourcing*. Then read the article to check your guess.**

*Crowd*: a large group of people *Outsourcing*: getting outside workers to do jobs for a business

*Crowdsourcing* is:

- A website about a particular topic.
- A large group of volunteers completing a task together.
- A free Internet encyclopedia.

### CROWDSOURCING

What can bring together a big crowd? A football game or a rock concert can fill a stadium with people. But big crowds also bring big problems to solve, like security or cleaning up after the event. The people in charge often outsource these jobs to security and cleaning companies.

Can you imagine a rock band asking the audience to volunteer to clean up before they leave? That is the basic idea of crowdsourcing – using a large group of volunteers to work together on a project. The word *crowdsourcing* is a combination of the words *crowd* and *outsource*.

Crowdsourced websites, such as wikis and social networking sites, are some of the most successful Internet organizations. Wikis offer millions of people free online information on a variety of topics. Almost 100,000 volunteers from around the world write and edit the topics in many different languages. Social networking websites also use crowdsourcing. They connect users to stories, ideas, opinions, and news, and they give people instant access to information from many sources. This information is often not available in traditional media such as news websites or TV news.

Wikis are some of the most visited websites in the world. However, many critics disapprove of their structure. They argue volunteers don't have the expertise to write about some topics. They also claim a lot of wiki articles are poorly written. Another issue is that wikis and social networking websites are only as useful as their network size. Some wikis and social networking websites fail because they do not have a big enough crowd to provide much interesting information.

Crowdsourcing has some problems. On the other hand, it is a useful way to complete large projects. It shows that when lots of individuals contribute a small amount of time and energy, it quickly adds up to a significant result.

**B Read the article again. Write *T* (true) or *F* (false) for each sentence. Then correct the false sentences.**

1. *Outsourcing* means using somebody inside a business to do work. ________
2. Wikis don't pay people to write articles for them. ________
3. Almost 10,000 people around the world write articles for wikis. ________
4. Social networking websites need large crowds to succeed. ________

## 2 Pros and cons

Writing **A Match each section of a short article to the correct sentence.**

| Section | Summary |
|---|---|
| 1. Introduction to the topic of crowdsourcing _b_ | a. Crowdsourcing has pros and cons, but it also has significant results. |
| 2. Advantages of crowdsourcing ____ | ✓b. *Crowdsourcing* means using a large group of volunteers to complete a project. |
| 3. Disadvantages of crowdsourcing ____ | c. Crowdsourced websites offer millions of people free information, news, and opinions often not available in traditional media. |
| 4. Conclusion ____ | d. However, information is not always correct on crowdsourced websites, and their crowds are not always large enough to be useful. |

**B Write a short article on a popular crowdsourcing website. Include an introduction, the advantages, the disadvantages, and a conclusion.**

____________ ____________ *is very popular these days*

## Unit 10 Progress chart

| What can you do? Mark the boxes.<br>✓ = I can . . .   ? = I need to review how to . . . | To review, go back to these pages in the Student's Book. |
|---|---|
| **Grammar**<br>☐ make comparisons with adjectives.<br>☐ use *more*, *less*, and *fewer* with nouns and verbs. | 98 and 99<br>101 |
| **Vocabulary**<br>☐ name at least 6 kinds of electronic communication.<br>☐ use at least 5 different phone expressions. | 97 and 98<br>100 and 101 |
| **Conversation strategies**<br>☐ interrupt and restart conversations on the phone.<br>☐ use *just* to soften things I say. | 102 and 103<br>103 |
| **Writing**<br>☐ write an article including the advantages and disadvantages of a topic, and a conclusion with my views. | 105 |

# Appearances

UNIT 11

## Lesson A Family traits

### 1 What's wrong?

Grammar and vocabulary **Look at the pictures. Correct the three mistakes in each description.**

1. Teresa is old. She's a little heavy. She's got long blond hair. She looks a lot like Megan. She's wearing a black sweater.

   *Teresa isn't old. She's young.*
   ____________________________________
   ____________________________________

2. Megan is young. She's slim with long straight hair. She looks a lot like Teresa. She's wearing a white sweater.

   ____________________________________
   ____________________________________
   ____________________________________

### 2 Do you look alike?

Grammar **Complete the conversation with the missing questions. Sometimes there is more than one correct answer.**

**Kari** Did you meet my brother Bob at the party last night? He's home for spring break.

**David** I'm not sure. Does he look like you? I mean, *do you look alike?*

**Kari** No, we look totally different.

**David** Huh. So, ____________________?

**Kari** He's six four. He's a lot taller than me.

**David** Wow. And ____________________?

**Kari** No, he doesn't. It's very curly. But it's blond like mine.

**David** Then it's not the guy I'm thinking of. ____________________?

**Kari** He's 21. So he's younger than me.

**David** Oh, OK. ____________________? Are they green?

**Kari** Yes, he's got green eyes. Oh, look. He's here now.

**David** Oh, him! So, ____________________?

**Kari** Actually, he takes after my mom. And I look like my dad.

## 3 A family portrait

Grammar and vocabulary | **Look at the picture and answer the questions.**

1. Who does Karen take after, Sharon or Dick? *She takes after Sharon.*
2. Who's got dark hair? __________
3. Do all the women have straight hair? __________
4. Do Kevin and Joey look alike? __________
5. Who do Kevin and Joey take after? __________

## About you

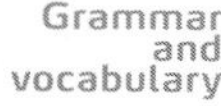

**Answer the questions with true information.**

1. How tall are you? Are you taller or shorter than your parents?
   *I'm taller than my mother, but I'm shorter than my father.*
2. Do you take after your father or your mother? How?
   __________
3. Who does your father take after, his mother or his father? How?
   __________
4. How many people have dark hair in your family? Does anyone have curly hair?
   __________
5. What color eyes do people in your family have?
   __________

## 1 What is it?

Vocabulary **A Read the clues and write the features.**

1. They can make a person's teeth straight. *braces*
2. It grows on a man's chin. ________
3. They are tiny braids close to a person's head. ________
4. People wear them to see better. ________
5. They have tiny holes for wearing earrings. ________
6. People who do weight training usually get this way. ________
7. They are little brown spots on a person's face or body. ________
8. It grows under a man's nose. ________
9. This is what we call men with no hair. ________
10. Some women paint them to make their hands look nice. ________
11. People with long hair often wear it in one of these to keep their hair out of the way. ________
12. This is your hairstyle if your hair is short and stands up. ________

**B Answer the questions with your own ideas and information.**

1. Do you think men should have pierced ears? *No, I don't. I don't think men should wear jewelry.*
   **or** *I think it's OK. Men wear rings and bracelets, so it's OK if they wear earrings, too.*
2. Do you know anyone with freckles? ________
3. Did you ever wear braces on your teeth? ________
4. Which is better, being muscular or being thin? Why? ________
5. How many people in the class wear their hair in a ponytail? Does anyone wear braids or cornrows? ________
6. Do you know anyone with a shaved head, a beard, or a mustache? ________
7. Do any of your friends have spiked hair? Are any of them bald? ________

## 2 Which one?

Grammar and vocabulary

**Look at the picture. Write a sentence about each student using the word given and one other descriptive phrase as in the example.**

1. A Which one is Lisa? (check her grades)
   B *Lisa is the one in the black jeans checking her grades.*
2. A Which one is Julio? (stand at the back)
   B ______________________________
3. A Which one is Mei-ling? (listen to music)
   B ______________________________
4. A Who is Luigi? (write an essay)
   B ______________________________
5. A What about Ivy, which one is she? (sit at the front)
   B ______________________________
6. A So which guy is Kareem? (wear a striped T-shirt)
   B ______________________________
7. A Which one is Anna? (talk to Kareem)
   B ______________________________
8. A Is Kazu here? Who is he? (read a book)
   B ______________________________

# Lesson C What's his name?

## 1 I can't remember

Conversation strategies

**Complete the conversations with the questions in the box.**

| What's his / her name?<br>What do you call it / them?<br>What do you call that thing / those things? |
|---|

1. **Katherine** Hey, Yong-joon, you're a big soccer fan. We're trying to remember the name of that famous Brazilian player. *What's his name?* __________

**Yong-joon** Do you mean Marcelo?

**Katherine** I don't know. He's got short hair, and it sticks up on top. __________________________

**Yong-joon** Spiked hair? Then it's not Marcelo. Maybe you're thinking of Neymar.

**Katherine** Hmm. And then we're trying to remember the name of the guy with long hair, you know he wears it in those long twisted . . . __________________________

**Yong-joon** Oh, you mean dreadlocks. You're thinking of Ronaldinho.

**Katherine** Yes, that's one of the players. So who's the other one?

**Yong-joon** I don't know. But you know, I think Ronaldinho looks different now. He often wears one of those wool hats . . . Oh, __________________________

**Katherine** Oh, a beanie. Really?

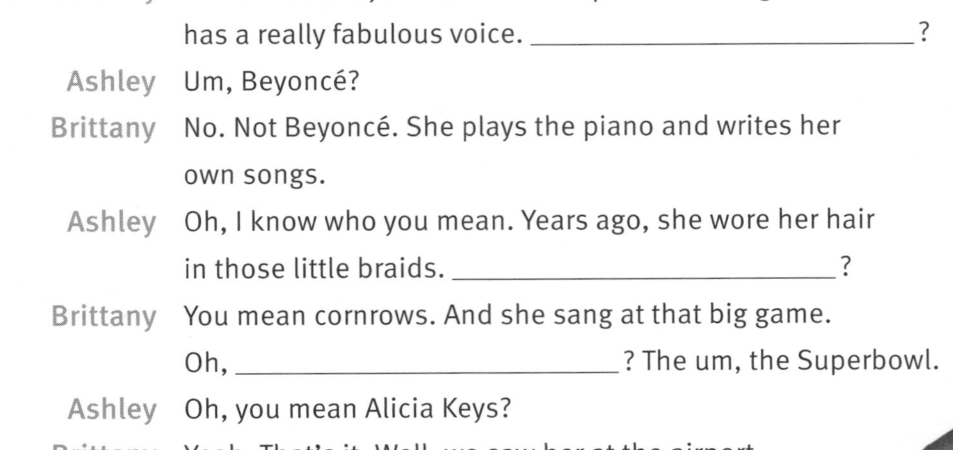

2. **Brittany** Guess who we just saw at the airport! That singer, she has a really fabulous voice. __________________________?

**Ashley** Um, Beyoncé?

**Brittany** No. Not Beyoncé. She plays the piano and writes her own songs.

**Ashley** Oh, I know who you mean. Years ago, she wore her hair in those little braids. __________________________?

**Brittany** You mean cornrows. And she sang at that big game. Oh, __________________________? The um, the Superbowl.

**Ashley** Oh, you mean Alicia Keys?

**Brittany** Yeah. That's it. Well, we saw her at the airport.

## 2 Oh, you mean . . .

Conversation strategies

**Who are they talking about? Respond using *You mean . . .* or *Do you mean . . .* ? Then match the pictures.**

1. A Who's that Mexican actress – the one who played Frida Kahlo in that movie?
   B *Oh, you mean Salma Hayek.* ___*d*___
2. A I really like those tennis players . . . what are their names? They're sisters with the cool tennis outfits.
   B ______________________ ____
3. A Do you want to go see that hip-hop band? You know, the one with the female singer?
   B ______________________ ____
4. A My friend just loves that golfer. You know – the really tall woman.
   B ______________________ ____
5. A I really like that actor – what's his name? – he's in *Pirates of the Caribbean*.
   B ______________________ ____

a Michelle Wie

b Black Eyed Peas

c Johnny Depp

d Salma Hayek

e Venus and Serena Williams

## 3 Describe it.

**Look at the pictures. Complete the descriptions without using the actual word(s). Then respond with *You mean . . .* or *Do you mean . . .* ?**

1. A My sister loves to wear *those fancy women's shoes. They make women look really tall.*
   B *Do you mean high heels?*
2. A My brother's hair ______________________
   ______________________
   B ______________________
3. A I just bought some of those pants with ______________________
   ______________________
   B ______________________
4. A My father has ______________________
   ______________________
   B ______________________

# Lesson D Changing fashions

## 1 Hair trends

Reading **A Look at the pictures. Then read the article. Match each picture with a decade.**

70s

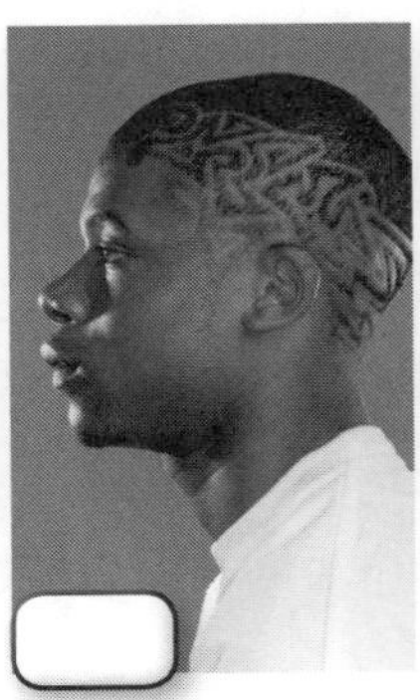

### Hairstyles through the decades...

Do you know how people wore their hair 10, 20, or 30 years ago? Look back at some of the popular hairstyles of the last few decades. There are some styles that come back again and again.

The 1950s were the beginning of the "rock 'n' roll" era. In the early '50s, men had short hair, but singer Elvis Presley changed all that when he combed his long hair into a "pompadour" and "duck tail." The ponytail was a popular hairstyle for young women.

The '60s was the decade of the Beatles, who caused a sensation when they grew their hair long – to their ears! In the late '60s and the early '70s, the "hippie look" was in style. Men and women grew their hair very long, and a lot of men had beards. The "Afro" was a popular hairstyle for African-Americans and anyone with curly hair or "perms."

Punk rockers shocked everyone with their multicolored, spiky hair in the '70s. Then in the late '70s and '80s, soap opera stars made "big hair" popular – women wore their hair very long, curly, and full.

The "new romantic" women of the '80s wore hairstyles from the 19th century – long curly hair and French braids. For many men, the "mullet" cut (short on top and long in the back) was the hairstyle to have.

In the '90s, dyed hair became stylish. Both men and women started changing the color of their hair or adding highlights. Some men began to bleach their hair blond.

In the 2000s, many women changed to a more "natural" look with long hair, similar to the 1970 hippie look. Some men had designs shaved into their hair; others had a textured or layered look.

So, what's going to be next? Look around you. Do you see any styles that are really "new"?

**B Read the article again. Write *T* (true) or *F* (false) for each sentence. Then correct the false sentences.**

1. Before Elvis Presley, guys wore their hair in a pompadour. _F_
2. In the '60s, the Beatles had very short hair. ____
3. In the '70s, curly hair and long hair were fashionable. ____
4. In the '90s, more people started to change the color of their hair. ____
5. In the 2000s, women started using more hair products than ever before. ____
6. Musicians and singers started some of the fashions in the last 50 years. ____

## 2 What's "in"?

Writing **A Read the article. Replace each underlined adjective and expression with a similar one in the box. Sometimes there is more than one correct answer.**

fashionable "in" in style "out" out of style popular the "in" thing ✓trendy

### Plan your new look!

You're ready to buy new clothes. But wait! Look in your own closet first. Find colors that are "~~in~~" *trendy* this season, and see if they match with clothes you already have. Look at the colorful clothes people are wearing. Black will always be fashionable, but it's no longer the only choice. Add some tops in strong colors, since they are the "in" thing this year.

Casual dress is slowly going out of style. For example, sportswear is not very popular these days. Your best bet is to buy classics that are going to be in style for a longer time. As for jeans, look for the trendy styles arriving in stores soon. Skinny jeans will soon be "out," so think carefully before buying.

Remember, you often need to try on a lot of different styles to get a look that is right for you. Don't forget to have fun!

**B Write a short article about new fashion trends using the expressions in the box above.**

## Unit 11 Progress chart

| | What can you do? Mark the boxes. ✓ = I can . . . ? = I need to review how to . . . | To review, go back to these pages in the Student's Book. |
|---|---|---|
| Grammar | ☐ use *have* and *have got* to describe people.<br>☐ use phrases with verb + *-ing* and prepositions to identify people. | 108 and 109<br>111 |
| Vocabulary | ☐ name at least 14 expressions and adjectives to describe people. | 110 and 111 |
| Conversation strategies | ☐ show that I'm trying to remember a word.<br>☐ use *You mean . . .* to help someone remember something. | 112 and 113<br>113 |
| Writing | ☐ use expressions to describe trends. | 115 |

# Looking ahead

UNIT 12

## Lesson A What's next?

### 1 Things that go together

Vocabulary | **Complete these sentences with the expressions in the box.**

| ask for a promotion | finish this course | get a master's degree | study abroad |
|---|---|---|---|
| become a millionaire | ✓have a baby | retire | travel around |

1. My brother and his wife are going to *have a baby* in September – I think they'll name her Nina.
2. My uncle might ______________ . He has his own business, and it's doing really well.
3. I think I'm ready for more responsibility at work. Maybe I'll ______________ .
4. My cousin already has a degree in business, and he's going to ______________ in economics this fall.
5. First, I want to ______________ , and then I might take a harder class.
6. It won't be easy for my mom to ______________ after working for 40 years.
7. My friends think it will be difficult to ______________ because all the classes will be in English.
8. My cousins invited me to ______________ Australia next summer, but I think it's going to be too expensive.

### 2 We might move!

Grammar | **Circle the correct verbs to complete the sentences.**

New Message

To: Sarah_P@cup.com
From: Rachel_J@cup.com
Subject: A big change!

Hi Sarah!

My dad recently got a promotion at work so in May we**'re going to move / will move** to Peru. I'm so excited because it **'ll be / is being** a big change in our lives. Everything is planned. We **will take / are going to take** a short vacation first – we **are going to visit / will visit** Machu Picchu. I'm a little scared, too, though. I'm 100% sure it **won't / might not** be easy to move to another country where the language is different. I can't speak Spanish, so I probably **am not making / won't make** new friends quickly. Also, my brother probably **won't come / might not come** with us. He's studying for his master's degree, and I don't think he **takes / will take** time off from school.

I think I **'ll be / 'm being** lonely at first. I'm trying hard to learn Spanish before we leave! I'm taking a class in the evenings. My teacher says that at the end of the course I **can / will** know enough Spanish to get around. I don't know. I'm just worried that I can understand her now, but when I'm in Peru, I **can't / won't** understand anyone!

Don't forget to write me.

Love,
Rachel xx

# 3 Planning ahead

Grammar and vocabulary

**Write two sentences about each picture. Use the words in parentheses and *be going to* or *will*. Sometimes there is more than one correct answer.**

1. Linda has definite plans for next year. She has a place in college.
   *She's going to study for a master's degree.*
   (study for a master's degree)
   *She isn't going to look for a job.*
   (not look for a job)

2. Steve's not sure about his plans for the summer. He hopes to go away.
   ______________________________
   (probably / go to Mexico)
   ______________________________
   (not be able / go for long)

3. Betty and Clive made plans to retire this year.
   ______________________________
   (retire in Arizona)
   ______________________________
   (not retire / in New Mexico)

4. Sheena's taking acting classes. She wants to be a movie star.
   ______________________________
   (be an actor)
   ______________________________
   (maybe / be a star)

5. Simon is thinking about being a teacher. His favorite subject is math.
   ______________________________
   (probably / teach math)
   ______________________________
   (probably / not teach English)

6. Tim and Laura are excited about the summer because Laura is pregnant.
   ______________________________
   (have a baby)
   ______________________________
   (probably / not take a vacation)

## 1 What do they do?

Vocabulary | **Write the names of the jobs under the pictures.**

## 2 What are your plans?

Grammar | **Complete the conversations with the correct form of the verbs.**

1. **Emily** How's your job going?
   **Beth** OK. It *'ll be* ('ll be / 's) better when I ________ ('ll get / get) my degree.
   **Emily** Oh really? I guess after you ________ ('ll graduate / graduate), you ________ ('ll earn / earn) more money.
   **Beth** That's right. And I ________ ('ll be / 'm) able to ask for a promotion, too if I ________ ('ll get / get) really good grades.
   **Emily** Well, I'm sure all that hard work in night school is worth it.
   **Beth** I hope so. If I ________ (don't / won't) pass the exams, I ________ ('ll leave / leave) and study full time.

2. **Adam** What are you going to do after we ________ (finish / will finish) college?
   **Neil** I'm not sure. I ________ ('ll / may) go to graduate school. How about you?
   **Adam** Before I ________ (make / 'll make) any decisions, I think I ________ (talk / 'll talk) to my parents and ask them for advice. If they can help me, I ________ ('ll start / start) my own business.
   **Neil** Sounds good. When your business ________ (is / will) successful, will you give me a job after I ________ (graduate / will graduate)?
   **Adam** Sure. If you ________ (ask / will ask) nicely!

## 3 About you

Grammar and vocabulary | **Complete the sentences with true information using *after*, *before*, *if*, or *when*.**

1. I'm sure my family will be really happy *when I get a master's degree*.
2. I may study ________.
3. I hope I'll be able to ________.
4. I might not get ________.
5. I guess I won't ________.
6. I'll probably earn a lot of money ________.
7. I'll be disappointed ________.
8. One day I might, ________.
9. I probably won't ________.
10. I'll be really pleased ________.

# Lesson C I'll drive.

## 1 Promises, promises

Conversation strategies

**A Complete the conversations with the responses in the box.**

| | |
|---|---|
| ✓ I'll make some salad. | If you want, I'll call and remind you. |
| I won't forget. | I'll call you at 5:30, just in case. |
| I'll wake up. | I'll lend you one. |

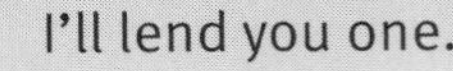

1. **Liam** Hey, Elaine! The class is having a picnic lunch on Saturday. Can you bring something?
   **Elaine** Sure. *I'll make some salad.*
   **Liam** Great! But don't forget the dressing like last time.
   **Elaine** ______________________ Well, I hope I won't.
   **Liam** ______________________
   **Elaine** Yeah, that might be good. Thanks.

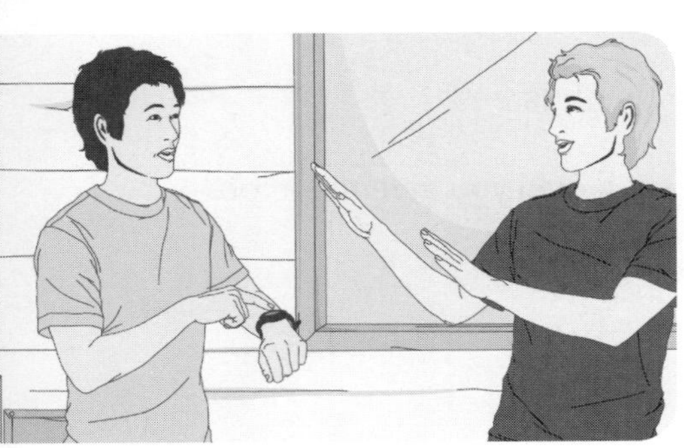

2. **Jerry** Remember to set your alarm tonight. We're leaving at 6:00 a.m.
   **Kevin** Uh, I lost my cell phone, but it's all right.
   **Jerry** I don't know. You might oversleep.
   **Kevin** Don't worry. ______________________
   **Jerry** You know, I have two alarm clocks. ______________________
   **Kevin** It's OK. Really. I always wake up early.
   **Jerry** ______________________
   **Kevin** OK, call me. Or maybe I should just stay at your place tonight. That way you won't worry!

**B Make an offer or promise using the words given.**

1. A Will you remember to call the plumber this afternoon?
   B Yes. *I won't forget.* (not forget)
2. A Oh, no! I forgot my cell phone. I have to call my brother for a ride home.
   B Don't worry. ____________ you home. (drive)
3. A I'm so hungry, and I left my lunch at home.
   B That's OK, ____________ some money. (lend)
4. A I don't know what kind of computer to buy.
   B If you want, ____________ you to decide. (help)
5. A Who's going to take care of the children while I go grocery shopping?
   B ____________ that, but I have to leave by 4:00. (do)
6. A I don't want to ride with you because you're never on time!
   B Don't worry. ____________ (not be late)

## 2 A surprise party

Conversation strategies | **Complete the conversation with the responses in the box.**

OK. Sure. I can send invitations online. I'll do that today.
All right. I can make one. Maybe a chocolate one?
OK. I will. Um, maybe you can call Lynn and tell her I'm organizing her birthday party!
Um . . . all right. I'll call and order – how many?
✓OK. I have plenty of space.
Um, all right. I'll think of something.

Nicole Tara, can we have Lynn's birthday party at your place this weekend? Mine's too small.
Tara *OK. I have plenty of space.*
Nicole And we should make a cake, but I'm not very good at baking. Can you make one?
Tara ______________________________
Nicole That sounds good. And would you mind doing the invitations, too? You're good at that stuff.
Tara ______________________________
Nicole And then we need a gift. Do you have any ideas? I mean, could you get her something?
Tara ______________________________
Nicole Thanks. I'll pay you for it. Oh, and one other thing. Should we order pizza or . . . ?
Tara ______________________________
Nicole Maybe four? Well, thanks Tara. I guess I'll go home. Call me if you need anything.
Tara ______________________________

## 3 A busy weekend

Conversation strategies | **Respond to the requests. Then make an offer using your own ideas.**

1. Could you make your special chicken dish for dinner? *All right. I'll make a salad, too.*
2. Can you help me buy a new tablet? ______________________________
3. Could you come with me to the gym on Saturday morning? ______________________________
4. Can you help me with my homework? ______________________________
5. Could you help me clean the kitchen? ______________________________

# In the future . . .

## Print it out!

Reading **A Read the article. Then circle the best title.**

Print Your Own Shoes    The Future of 3-D Printing    Building New Homes

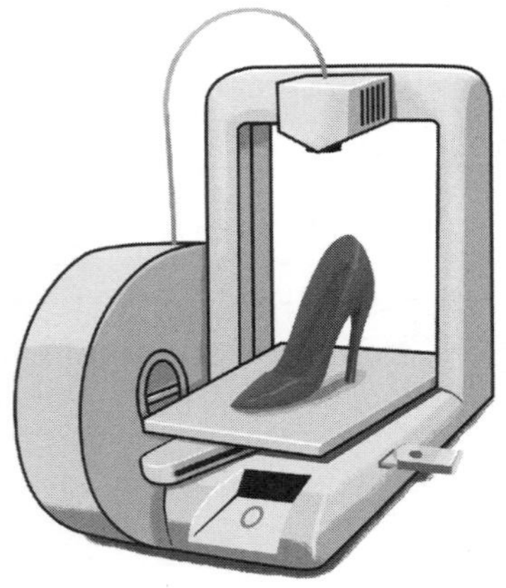

Imagine you're getting ready for a night out. First, you go online and pick out a pair of shoes. Second, you choose the size, style, and color. Next, you download the design and "print" the shoes. Finally, you put on your new shoes, and you're ready to walk out the door.

You may think that's impossible, and you might be right. There are some three-dimensional, or 3-D, printers in the world today, but you can't print out shoes quite yet. However, scientists believe 3-D printing will become common in the future.

Today, designers and engineers use 3-D printers to create high-tech models out of different materials, like plastic, metal, glass – even chocolate! They design the object in 3-D on a computer. Then a 3-D printer builds the object one layer at a time. These models help engineers test and improve designs before they make the real thing.

In the future, businesses will be able to print the real thing themselves. For example, when machines break down, companies will be able to print replacement parts and fix the machines the same day. Productivity will increase because workers won't have to wait for new parts to arrive. Another example is medical equipment. Doctors around the world will be able to simply print the items they need, and medical care will greatly improve!

As 3-D printers become more affordable, they will completely change shopping as we know it. Many scientists imagine an online marketplace where you will shop for designs. Then you will be able to print out footwear, jewelry, glasses, and other common objects in the comfort of your own home.

You might have a 3-D printer at home or work one day. What kinds of things could you print?

**B Circle the correct responses to complete the sentences.**

1. Printing your own shoes **will certainly / might** be possible in the future.
2. It **is / isn't** possible to use a 3-D printer to make things out of chocolate.
3. Right now, designers use 3-D printers to **make designs better / sell their designs**.
4. If companies have 3-D printers, they will be able to **test / repair** their own machines.
5. Engineers think that 3-D printers will become **more expensive / cheaper**.
6. In the future, 3-D printers **will / won't** change the way we buy personal items.

# 2 Life in the future

Writing

**A Read the paragraph. Add *First*, *Second*, *Next*, and *Finally* to the paragraph to list the examples. Change the punctuation.**

Blog

It is not easy to live in some big cities. For example, there are problems with traffic and pollution. However, 20 years from now, many of these cities may be better and cleaner. First, they will have better public transportation systems, and people won't need to drive cars. Also, there won't be many traffic jams or parking problems. There will be more open spaces and parks. People will be able to walk and cycle and spend time outdoors. The air will be cleaner because there will be fewer cars, and more cars will be electric. Industries will probably be cleaner and more efficient because solar power and wind power will be more popular. With these changes, big cities will be more attractive places to live.

**B Write a short article about one of these topics. Use *First*, *Second*, *Next*, and *Finally* to list examples within the article.**

- the ideal city of the future
- health in the future
- everyday life in the future
- the environment in the future

## Unit 12 Progress chart

| | What can you do? Mark the boxes. ✓ = I can . . . ? = I need to review how to . . . | To review, go back to these pages in the Student's Book. |
|---|---|---|
| Grammar | ☐ use *will*, *may*, and *might* to talk about the future.<br>☐ use the present continuous and *going to* for the future.<br>☐ use the simple present in clauses with *if*, *when*, *after*, and *before* to refer to the future. | 118 and 119<br>118 and 119<br>121 |
| Vocabulary | ☐ name at least 8 new expressions for work, study, or life plans.<br>☐ name at least 15 different occupations. | 118 and 119<br>120 and 121 |
| Conversation strategies | ☐ use *I'll* to make offers and promises.<br>☐ use *All right* and *OK* to agree to do something. | 122 and 123<br>123 |
| Writing | ☐ use *first*, *second*, *next*, and *finally* to list ideas. | 125 |

# Illustration credits

**Ken Batelman:** 42, 44 **Lisa Blackshear:** 24 **Domninic Bugatto:** 14, 34, 82, 83 **Cambridge University Press:** 25, 27, 49, 52 **Daniel Chen:** 6, 94 **Matt Collins:** 40 **Chuck Gonzales:** 19, 29, 67, 75, 85, 96 **Frank Montagna:** 10, 22, 30, 58, 59, 69, 78 **Marilena Perilli:** 5, 66, 70, 85 **Greg White:** 20, 47, 62, 63, 91 **Terry Wong:** 2, 3, 28, 55, 61

# Photo credits

**4** *(clockwise from top left)* ©JupiterImages; ©Monkey Business Images/Shutterstock; ©Alan Thornton/Getty Images; ©YURI KADOBNOV/AFP/Getty Images; ©Ocean/Corbis; ©Punchstock **8** ©Kjpargeter/Shutterstock **11** ©Image Source/SuperStock **12** *(top row, left to right)* ©Henry Diltz/Corbis; ©Charles Sykes/Associated Press; ©Matt Kent/WireImage/Getty Images; ©Frank Micelotta/Getty Images *(top row, left to right)* ©Barros & Barros/Getty Images; ©Tim Mosenfelder/Corbis; ©Al Bello/Getty Images; ©Peter Kramer/NBC/NBCU Photo Bank via Getty Images **13** *(top to bottom)* ©Jason Merritt/Getty Images For BET; ©Jon Kopaloff/FilmMagic/Getty Images **15** *(left to right)* ©Thinkstock; ©Sebastien Starr/Getty Images **16** *(background)* ©tdixon8875/Shutterstock **18** *(top to bottom)* ©Image Source/Getty Images; ©Digital Vision/Getty Images **21** *(clockwise from top left)* ©Mary Kate Denny/PhotoEdit; ©Dana White/PhotoEdit; ©Thinkstock; ©Jose Luis Pelaez Inc./Corbis **25** ©Punchstock **26** *(top to bottom)* ©Gregg DeGuire/WireImage/Getty Images; ©Russ Einhorn 2004/Russ Einhorn/Splash News/Newscom; ©Jason LaVeris/FilmMagic/Getty Images; ©Gregg DeGuire/WireImage/Getty Images; ©Jason LaVeris/FilmMagic/Getty Images; ©Alex Livesey - FIFA/FIFA via Getty Images **31** ©Keren Su/China Span/Alamy **32** *(top to bottom)* ©Anna-Mari West/Shutterstock; ©Africa Studio/Shutterstock **35** ©Michael Newman/PhotoEdit **39** ©Michael Newman/PhotoEdit **46** *(left to right)* ©Blend Images/SuperStock; ©Andersen Ross/Getty Images **48** *(top to bottom)* ©Joel Arem/Getty Images; ©HUGHES Herve/hemis.fr/Getty Images; ©Andrew Watson/Getty Images **50** ©Ralph Lee Hopkins/Getty Images **51** ©Dave Fleetham/Pacific Stock - Design Pics/SuperStock *(background)* ©sdecoret/Shutterstock **53** *(left to right)* ©Thinkstock; ©Jupiterimages/Thinkstock **54** *(top to bottom)* ©Greg Elms/Getty Images; ©Michael Goldman/Masterfile **56** *(left to right)* ©Purcell Team/Alamy; ©DIOMEDIA/Alamy; ©Peter Grant/Getty Images **57** ©Trish Punch/Getty Images **64** Photos Courtesy of Poezenboot **68** *(top to bottom)* ©Thinkstock; ©Punchstock **76** *(left to right)* ©PhotoInc/Getty Images; ©Kablonk/SuperStock **77** ©Dougal Waters/Getty Images **80** ©Raoul Minsart/Masterfile *(background)* ©Kjpargeter/Shutterstock **82** ©David Lees/Getty Images **84** *(top to bottom)* ©Punchstock; ©largeformat4x5/Getty Images; ©Seth Resnick/Science Faction/SuperStock **86** *(top to bottom)* ©Maximiliano Failla/AFP/Getty Images; ©Shaun Botterill - FIFA/FIFA via Getty Images; ©STR/AFP/Getty Images; ©s_bukley/Shutterstock **87** *(top to bottom)* ©David Cannon/Getty Images; ©Ric Francis/Associated Press; ©DFree/Shutterstock; ©cinemafestival/Shutterstock; ©Clive Brunskill/Getty Images; ©Elnur/Shutterstock; ©Amos Morgan/Thinkstock; ©Thinkstock; ©Jupiterimages/Thinkstock **88** *(left to right)* ©imagebroker.net/SuperStock; ©Iain McKell/Getty Images; ©Masterfile; ©Nick Dolding/Getty Images; ©Ellen Stagg/Getty Images; ©Thinkstock *(background)* ©alex.makarova/Shutterstock **92** *(left column, top to bottom)* ©Punchstock; ©George Doyle/Thinkstock; ©George Doyle & Ciaran Griffin/Thinkstock; ©Jack Hollingsworth/Getty Images; ©Corbis; ©Thinkstock *(middle column, top to bottom)* ©Jupiterimages/Thinkstock; ©Thinkstock; ©Jeff Greenberg/PhotoEdit; ©David Young-Wolff/PhotoEdit; ©Michael Newman/PhotoEdit; ©Tetra Images/Getty Images *(right column, top to bottom)* ©Tom Carter/PhotoEdit; ©Jupiterimages/Thinkstock; ©Thinkstock; ©Flying Colours Ltd/Getty Images; ©Robin Nelson/PhotoEdit; ©JupiterImages

# Text credits

While every effort has been made, it has not always been possible to identify the sources of all the material used, or to trace all copyright holders. If any omissions are brought to our notice, we will be happy to include the appropriate acknowledgements on reprinting.

# The top 500 spoken words

This is a list of the top 500 words in spoken North American English. It is based on a sample of four and a half million words of conversation from the Cambridge International Corpus. The most frequent word, *I*, is at the top of the list.

1. I
2. and
3. the
4. you
5. uh
6. to
7. a
8. that
9. it
10. of
11. yeah
12. know
13. in
14. like
15. they
16. have
17. so
18. was
19. but
20. is
21. it's
22. we
23. huh
24. just
25. oh
26. do
27. don't
28. that's
29. well
30. for
31. what
32. on
33. think
34. right
35. not
36. um
37. or
38. my
39. be
40. really
41. with
42. he
43. one
44. are
45. this
46. there
47. I'm
48. all
49. if
50. no
51. get
52. about
53. at
54. out
55. had
56. then
57. because
58. go
59. up
60. she
61. when
62. them
63. can
64. would
65. as
66. me
67. mean
68. some
69. good
70. got
71. OK
72. people
73. now
74. going
75. were
76. lot
77. your
78. time
79. see
80. how
81. they're
82. kind
83. here
84. from
85. did
86. something
87. too
88. more
89. very
90. want
91. little
92. been
93. things
94. an
95. you're
96. said
97. there's
98. I've
99. much
100. where
101. two
102. thing
103. her
104. didn't
105. other
106. say
107. back
108. could
109. their
110. our
111. guess
112. yes
113. way
114. has
115. down
116. we're
117. any

# The top 500 spoken words

118. he's
119. work
120. take
121. even
122. those
123. over
124. probably
125. him
126. who
127. put
128. years
129. sure
130. can't
131. pretty
132. gonna
133. stuff
134. come
135. these
136. by
137. into
138. went
139. make
140. than
141. year
142. three
143. which
144. home
145. will
146. nice
147. never
148. only
149. his
150. doing
151. cause
152. off
153. I'll
154. maybe
155. real
156. why
157. big
158. actually
159. she's
160. day
161. five
162. always
163. school
164. look
165. still
166. around
167. anything
168. kids
169. first
170. does
171. need
172. us
173. should
174. talking
175. last
176. thought
177. doesn't
178. different
179. money
180. long
181. used
182. getting
183. same
184. four
185. every
186. new
187. everything
188. many
189. before
190. though
191. most
192. tell
193. being
194. bit
195. house
196. also
197. use
198. through
199. feel
200. course
201. what's
202. old
203. done
204. sort
205. great
206. bad
207. we've
208. another
209. car
210. true
211. whole
212. whatever
213. twenty
214. after
215. ever
216. find
217. care
218. better
219. hard
220. haven't
221. trying
222. give
223. I'd
224. problem
225. else
226. remember
227. might
228. again
229. pay
230. try
231. place
232. part
233. let
234. keep
235. children
236. anyway
237. came
238. six
239. family
240. wasn't
241. talk
242. made
243. hundred
244. night
245. call
246. saying

# The top 500 spoken words

247. dollars
248. live
249. away
250. either
251. read
252. having
253. far
254. watch
255. week
256. mhm
257. quite
258. enough
259. next
260. couple
261. own
262. wouldn't
263. ten
264. interesting
265. am
266. sometimes
267. bye
268. seems
269. heard
270. goes
271. called
272. point
273. ago
274. while
275. fact
276. once
277. seen
278. wanted
279. isn't
280. start
281. high
282. somebody
283. let's
284. times
285. guy
286. area
287. fun
288. they've
289. you've
290. started
291. job
292. says
293. play
294. usually
295. wow
296. exactly
297. took
298. few
299. child
300. thirty
301. buy
302. person
303. working
304. half
305. looking
306. someone
307. coming
308. eight
309. love
310. everybody
311. able
312. we'll
313. life
314. may
315. both
316. type
317. end
318. least
319. told
320. saw
321. college
322. ones
323. almost
324. since
325. days
326. couldn't
327. gets
328. guys
329. god
330. country
331. wait
332. yet
333. believe
334. thinking
335. funny
336. state
337. until
338. husband
339. idea
340. name
341. seven
342. together
343. each
344. hear
345. help
346. nothing
347. parents
348. room
349. today
350. makes
351. stay
352. mom
353. sounds
354. change
355. understand
356. such
357. gone
358. system
359. comes
360. thank
361. show
362. thousand
363. left
364. friends
365. class
366. already
367. eat
368. small
369. boy
370. paper
371. world
372. best
373. water
374. myself
375. run

## The top 500 spoken words

376. they'll
377. won't
378. movie
379. cool
380. news
381. number
382. man
383. basically
384. nine
385. enjoy
386. bought
387. whether
388. especially
389. taking
390. sit
391. book
392. fifty
393. months
394. women
395. month
396. found
397. side
398. food
399. looks
400. summer
401. hmm
402. fine
403. hey
404. student
405. agree
406. mother
407. problems
408. city
409. second
410. definitely
411. spend
412. happened
413. hours
414. war
415. matter
416. supposed
417. worked
418. company
419. friend
420. set
421. minutes
422. morning
423. between
424. music
425. close
426. leave
427. wife
428. knew
429. pick
430. important
431. ask
432. hour
433. deal
434. mine
435. reason
436. credit
437. dog
438. group
439. turn
440. making
441. American
442. weeks
443. certain
444. less
445. must
446. dad
447. during
448. lived
449. forty
450. air
451. government
452. eighty
453. wonderful
454. seem
455. wrong
456. young
457. places
458. girl
459. happen
460. sorry
461. living
462. drive
463. outside
464. bring
465. easy
466. stop
467. percent
468. hand
469. gosh
470. top
471. cut
472. computer
473. tried
474. gotten
475. mind
476. business
477. anybody
478. takes
479. aren't
480. question
481. rather
482. twelve
483. phone
484. program
485. without
486. moved
487. gave
488. yep
489. case
490. looked
491. certainly
492. talked
493. beautiful
494. card
495. walk
496. married
497. anymore
498. you'll
499. middle
500. tax